Advertising in a Recession: The Benefits of Investing for the Long Term

Edited by

Patrick Barwise

First published 1999 by NTC Publications Ltd
Farm Road, Henley-on-Thames
Oxfordshire RG9 1EJ, United Kingdom
Telephone: +44 (0) 1491 411000
Facsimile: +44 (0) 1491 571188

A CIP catalogue record for this book is available from the British Library

ISBN 1-84116-043-1
Copyright © Centre for Marketing, London Business School
Cover picture: The Sower by Jean-François Millet (1814–75). Museum of Fine Arts, Boston,
Massachusetts, MA, USA/Bridgeman Art Library

Typeset by Marie Doherty
Printed and bound in Great Britain by Biddles Ltd, Guildford and King's Lynn

Executive Summary

In an ideal world, economies and markets would grow steadily and predictably. In the real world, growth fluctuates, often unpredictably. The danger is that, when times are tough, panic sets in and budgets are cut in order to meet short-term financial targets. This book – prepared at a time when most economies and markets are growing – is an attempt to address this issue dispassionately while the pressure is off.

Specifically, this book aims to help senior managers, including CEOs and senior finance managers, decide how much to spend on advertising when the economy slows down. Its underlying theme is the importance of having and sticking with a clear long-term strategy for the brand.

The introductory chapter, "Advertising for Long-Term Shareholder Value", sets the stage. It argues that:

- Regardless of economic conditions, every firm needs a clear strategy for its major brands, based on the classic marketing principles of segmentation, competitor analysis, targeting, and positioning. Advertising strategy, including how much to invest, should be an integral part of this wider strategy.
- These principles still apply when the economy slows down, although details, such as the relative importance of different segments, may change.
- The financial markets look for long-term shareholder value, not just short-term financial performance. If a firm has a convincing strategy and good investor relations it can keep investing in marketing and product innovation even if the economy slows down, without a negative reaction from shareholders.

Part One reprints some of the best previous research and commentary on advertising in a recession. Although this is a difficult research area, the evidence is that generally:

- The most successful companies maximise long-term shareholder value by maintaining their advertising investment when the economy slows down and weaker competitors cut back.
- This enables them to build market share at lower cost than when the total market is growing.

– Any reduction in these firms' short-term financial performance is typically soon outweighed by their increased revenue and profit growth when economic conditions improve.

In Part Two, these general principles and findings are illustrated in six case histories of advertising in a recession, introduced and edited by Marilyn Baxter (Saatchi & Saatchi). The six cases, selected from the winners of IPA Advertising Effectiveness Awards, are all good examples of advertising strategy, planning and execution during a recession, and of best-practice campaign evaluation. Although every case (like every brand) is unique, they are loosely grouped under three headings, each representing a generic positive response to economic slowdown:

– Look for new creative or targeting opportunities (Renault Clio, Whipsnade Wild Animal Park, De Beers).
– Strengthen your market position against weaker rivals (Barclaycard).
– Keep going, i.e. hold firm to your long-term strategy (Nescafé Gold Blend, BMW).

In one sense, the need for a distinctive, credible strategy has nothing to do with the state of the economy, but an economic slowdown can bring the issues to a head. This can be the opportunity to sharpen the discussion about marketing strategy in general. Deciding how much to spend on advertising should be just a part of that wider discussion.

Acknowledgements

I would like to thank the authors of the six readings in Part One for allowing us to edit and reprint their work; ITV for supporting the book; and the Advertising Association (AA), Institute of Practitioners in Advertising (IPA) and Incorporated Society of British Advertisers (ISBA) for the further support which has enabled us to broaden its scope and its dissemination.

The book has benefited greatly from the guidance and practical support of Dyan Clements and John Hardie (ITV), Andrew Brown and Mike Waterson (AA), and Ian Bell and Sue Moseley (TSMS).

I would also like to thank Marilyn Baxter (Saatchi & Saatchi) for her excellent selection and editing of the cases in Part Two; Liz Hussey, (Saatchi & Saatchi) for her helpfulness and quick responses to tight deadlines; Jane Mole and Lucy Reeve (London Business School) for their efficient management of what turned out to be a bigger and more complex project than we expected; and Matthew Coombs (NTC Publications) for getting the book out so quickly.

Patrick Barwise
London Business School
May 1999

Advertising for Long-Term Shareholder Value[1]

Patrick Barwise[2]

'I was asked what I thought about the recession. I thought about it and decided not to take part.'

Sam Walton, Founder of Wal-Mart[3]

In this chapter I first suggest a general framework for discussing how much to spend on advertising, including when the economy slows down. The proposed framework puts particular emphasis on (i) the distinction between short- and long-term effects and (ii) shareholders' likely reaction to a firm increasing, maintaining, or cutting advertising investment. This leads to five financial/economic questions which management should ask about any brand in order to decide how much to spend on advertising. The first three are general, regardless of economic conditions. The last two focus on the impact of an economic slowdown. I then briefly review what we do and do not know about each question from the wider research literature. The key points are that:

1. For most brands, it should be possible to quantify – at least roughly – the impact of advertising expenditure ('Adspend') on short-term financial performance.
2. The demonstrable short-term impact of advertising on sales (or margins) varies widely but in most cases it is not enough to cover the cost of the advertising.
3. In addition to its short-term effects, however, advertising can contribute to long-term shareholder value by increasing 'brand equity', ie the brand's ability to support a high market share, a premium price, and profitable brand extensions.

1. I am extremely grateful to Tim Ambler, Simon Broadbent, Bruce Hardie and Sriraman Venkataraman for helpful comments on earlier drafts of this chapter.
2. Patrick Barwise is Professor of Management and Marketing, and Director of the Centre for Marketing, at London Business School. He is also Deputy Chairman of Consumers' Association, and Joint Managing Editor of Business Strategy Review.
3. David Muir and Simeon Duckworth, Come the Fall, London: Ogilvy & Mather, 1998, p24.

4. The most successful firms do not allow short-term economic conditions to make them abandon their strategy. Instead, they typically maximise long-term shareholder value by maintaining or increasing their Adspend when the economy slows down and their weaker competitors cut back.
5. Any reduction in these firms' short-term financial performance is, in most cases, soon outweighed by their increased revenue and profit growth when economic conditions improve.
6. Contrary to widespread belief, the financial markets do look for long-term shareholder value, not just short-term financial performance. The markets are also willing to be convinced of the value of brand equity and other intangibles, even if they are sceptical of our ability to quantify this value (never mind the specific long-term contribution of advertising).
7. In this context, shareholder reactions depend crucially on the credibility of the firm's strategy, communicated through its actions, its financial statements and other corporate communications, and directly by the top management team.

The final section reviews the argument and concludes with three strategic options for advertising during a recession.

1 A general decision framework

Figure 1 shows a simple general model of the relationship between advertising expenditure (Adspend), short-term financial performance, expected long-term shareholder value, and shareholder reaction.
This model is enormously simplified. It excludes:

1. Economic conditions (discussed shortly)
2. All marketing variables apart from Adspend (itself reduced to a simple financial quantity, regardless of the aims or quality of the strategy and execution)
3. Competition (relative strength, market share and positioning; likely competitive response – a crucial area which few firms analyse well)
4. Intermediate effects (eg brand awareness, consumer attitudes, brand loyalty, trade presence, volume versus margin, etc.)
5. Reverse links (eg a negative shareholder reaction causing management to reduce Adspend).

Despite being so simplified, the model captures the main financial/economic variables in advertising decisions:

- Adspend
- Short-term financial performance (ie profit or cash flow up to, say, two years)
- Expected long-term shareholder value (ie the present value of expected cash flows discounted at the weighted average cost of capital)
- shareholder reaction (the impact on the financial market value of the firm).

This model has two important features. First, it distinguishes between short-term and long-term financial performance: these are very different from each other, involve different research and estimation approaches, and can respond very differently to changes in Adspend. Second, the model includes shareholder reaction as an explicit variable, rather than a hidden influence on decision-making. One benefit is to encourage dialogue within the management team, especially between the finance and marketing people.

To some readers, this may seem a laborious business-school way of stating the blindingly obvious. The anecdotal evidence is that such readers are mistaken. Few management teams have a clear, shared understanding of their situation in terms of Figure 1. More likely, they assume that their ability to invest for the long term is severely constrained because they also assume that the financial markets are short-sightedly fixated on short-term financial performance.

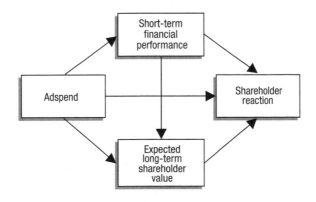

FIGURE 1: A SIMPLE GENERAL MODEL

The Impact of an Economic Slowdown

What about the impact of recession? Figure 1 presents a general framework which each firm must apply to its particular brand(s) and for the particular economic conditions expected at the time of the decision. An economic slowdown may raise further issues which may need to be taken into account.

2 Five questions for your brand

The general framework of Figure 1, together with the additional issue of economic slowdown, suggests five questions that management should ask for each specific brand. The first three are general, the last two specific to periods of actual or expected recession:

Q1   What is the impact of Adspend on short-term financial performance?

Q2   What is the impact of Adspend on expected long-term shareholder value?

Q3   What is the combined impact of Adspend, short-term financial performance, and expected long-term shareholder value on shareholder reaction?

Q4   What is the impact of an economic slowdown on the short-term and long-term profitability of advertising?

Q5   What is the impact of an economic slowdown on shareholder reactions to the other variables to Figure 1?

Although each of these questions should be addressed for each specific brand, there is some evidence in the literature about the general patterns.

Evidence on Short- and Long-Term Advertising Effects (Q1, Q2)

A full review of research on the first two questions is beyond the scope of this book. The research is both extensive and controversial, including the very concept of general patterns. Nevertheless, I believe we can safely draw the following conclusions:[4]

---

4. These are my personal conclusions, but in reaching them I have been helped by Sriram Venkataraman, who kindly reviewed the most recent research for me. The most up-to-date and comprehensive review of the literature on advertising effects is Demetrios Vakratas and Tim Ambler, 'How advertising works: what do we really know?', Journal of Marketing, 1999. The classic single-source studies in the US were summarised in Magid M. Abraham and Leonard M. Lodish, 'Getting the most out of advertising and promotion', Harvard Business Review, May–June 1990. The best study on advertising/promotion profitability is Kamel Jedidic, Carl F. Mela and Sunil Gupta, 'Managing advertising and promotion for long-run profitability', Marketing Science, 18, 1, 1999, 1-22 (warning: this is a somewhat technical paper).

Advertising for Long-Term Shareholder Value

1. For most brands, it should be possible to quantify – at least roughly – the impact of Adspend on short-term financial performance.

2. For an accurate assessment of this impact, one should ideally have: 'single-source' data (where advertising exposure and buying behaviour are measured for the same homes or individuals); experimentally controlled media weights in different areas or households; and a substantial sample size or evidence accumulated across several experiments (for precision and reliability). The most important of these three is probably the second – experimental control.

3. Studies using these methods show that the impact of advertising on short-term financial performance is extremely varied but usually negative. That is, the demonstrable short-term impact of advertising on sales (or margins) is positive but in most cases not enough to cover the cost of advertising. Two further results are that (i) for established packaged-goods brands, the cumulative sales impact over three years is roughly double the impact over one year, and (ii) advertising is more cost-effective when combined with product improvements.

4. In addition to its short-term effects, over the long term advertising can increase 'brand equity', ie the brand's ability to support a high market share, a premium price, and profitable brand extensions.[5] This, in turn, can lead to increased long-term shareholder value.

5. However, it has not been possible (and probably never will be) to pin down the precise contribution to brand equity and long-term profitability of advertising as a separate factor.

6. What we can realistically aim for is informed discussion of the short- and long-term value of advertising for a particular brand, based on clear advertising strategy and planning backed up with good metrics, models and research. The IPA cases included in Part Two illustrate this process at its best.

---

5. An exception is advertising which focuses on price: this tends to reduce brand equity. There is also growing evidence that price promotions reduce brand equity over the long term.

Evidence on Shareholder Reactions to Adspend, Short-Term Financial Performance, Expected Long-Term Shareholder Value and Economic Slowdown (Q3, Q5)

This, too, is a complex and controversial area beyond the scope of this book. However, I believe we can say the following:[6]

1. Most of the time, both institutional and individual shareholders are seeking to maximise long-term shareholder value. However, they cannot observe this directly and do not have free access to managers' expectations.
2. Financial markets are not systematically short-termist. They do, however, respond to changes in short-term financial performance as signals of changes in managers' expectations of long-term shareholder value.
3. The financial markets often attribute substantial value to brand equity and other intangible assets, beyond short-term financial performance. (At the time of writing, the US stock-market is placing sky-high valuations on Internet stocks, some of which do not even have revenues, never mind earnings.)
4. The anecdotal evidence is that the markets do not directly monitor Adspend, but would welcome fuller, systematic disclosure of marketing investments and other measures of brand stewardship.
5. Again anecdotally, the main determinant of shareholder reaction is analysts' and investors' belief in the credibility of the management team and its strategy. The issue for management is therefore to have a clear, convincing strategy and to communicate it to the financial community, subject to the constraints of commercial confidentiality[7] and insider trading regulations.

---

6. For general background, see S. Keane, Stock Exchange Efficiency: Theory, Evidence and Implications, Oxford: Philip Allen, 1983, and Richard A. Brealey and Stewart C. Myers, Principles of Corporate Finance, McGraw Hill, 5th edn, 1996. Specific studies include Paul R. Marsh, Short-termism on Trial, London Business School 1990; Carol J. Simon and Mary W. Sullivan, 'The measurement and determinants of brand equity: a financial approach' Marketing Science, 12, 1, 1993, 28-52; David A. Aaker and Robert Jacobson, 'The financial information content of perceived quality', Journal of Marketing Research, 31, 1994, 191-201; The Brand Finance Report 1998 (Teddington, Middx: Brand Finance Ltd); David Muir and Simeon Duckworth, Come the Fall, London: Ogilvy & Mather, 1998; Mary E. Barth, Michael B. Clement, George Foster and Ron Kasznik, 'Brand values and capital market valuation', Review of Accounting Studies, forthcoming.

7. In some cases, signalling your intent (eg to focus on a particular target market or brand positioning) may actually encourage competitors to concentrate their efforts elsewhere.

6. If the economy slows down, most shareholders are still concerned with long-term shareholder value but the 'financial climate' gets more difficult, putting more emphasis on short-term financial performance.

7. Anecdotally, firms seek to smooth reported earnings by building up 'hidden' reserves during the good times and drawing on them during bad times. Analysts and investors know this, increasing their sensitivity to decreases in reported short-term financial performance (see (2) above).

The Impact of Recession on the Short- and Long-term Profitability of Advertising (Q4)

To my knowledge, there has been no academic research on this, the central topic of this book. There has, however, been extensive practitioner research, represented by the readings in Part One.

This research compares (i) the performance of a group of firms which increased or maintained advertising during a recession against (ii) the performance of another group of firms which cut back.

The clear pattern is that the first group tends to increase its market share during the economic slowdown and then outperforms the second group (in terms of both sales and profit growth) during the recovery. What is unclear is the extent to which this performance difference reflects other variations between the two groups of firms (eg that the first group is simply better and/or stronger) or the timing of the study (eg that it starts just as firms in the first group have new products almost ready to launch, when advertising is both more necessary and more profitable than usual).

Despite these caveats, the research shows that:

1. The most successful firms maximise long-term shareholder value by maintaining or increasing their Adspend when the economy slows down and their weaker rivals cut back.

2. This enables them (on average) to build market share faster and at less cost than when the total market is growing. One reason for this is that, if weaker competitors cut back, those who maintain (or increase) their Adspend achieve a higher 'share of voice' (ie their share of total category advertising goes up). Another factor is that, if the slowdown affects the whole media market, media rates may be more negotiable, so that a given Adspend may buy more impacts (eg TV ratings).

3. Although maintaining or increasing Adspend when the economy slows down will, on average, reduce the firm's short-term financial performance, the effects seem to be quite

limited. The evidence is that this short-term reduction is soon outweighed by the firm's increased revenue and profit growth when economic conditions improve.

In addition to these general effects, an economic slowdown can have many market-specific effects as consumers trade down to lower-priced products and brands, smaller pack sizes and money-saving applications, or as expenditure shifts between market segments. For instance, if interest rates go up, younger families with mortgages suffer a reduction in their disposable income, but older people with net savings see their income rise. As always in marketing, any change can bring opportunities as well as problems, and these should be exploited before the competition spots them.

3 Conclusions: three positive strategies

Briefly summarising the argument of this chapter:

- Regardless of economic conditions, every firm needs a clear strategy for its major brands based on the classic marketing principles of segmentation, competitor analysis, targeting, and positioning. Advertising strategy, including how much to invest, should be an integral part of this strategy.
- These principles still apply when the economy slows down, although details, such as the relative importance of different segments, may change.
- Contrary to widespread belief, the financial markets look for long-term shareholder value, not just short-term financial performance. If a firm has a convincing strategy (and good investor relations) it can keep investing in marketing and product innovation even if the economy slows down, without a negative reaction from shareholders.

In the context of an economic slowdown, we can classify brand strategies into three brand types:

1. Look for new creative, media or targeting opportunities.
2. Strengthen your market position against weaker rivals.
3. Keep going, ie hold firm to your long-term strategy.

While any specific strategy may combine elements of all three of these, I believe that the most powerful over the long term is (3). This is well encapsulated in the Sam Walton quotation at the start of the chapter. We return to these strategies in Part Two and in the brief Conclusions chapter.

PART ONE

Previous Research and Commentary

Introduction to Part One

Patrick Barwise

Proving the effects – especially the long-term effects – of advertising is notoriously difficult. Proving the specific benefits of advertising in a recession is even harder. As far as I know, there has been no previous academic research on this topic. There has, however, been a substantial amount of research and commentary by practitioners. The six readings reprinted here represent some of the best examples.

Although it is unrealistic to expect definitive proof, these readings provide strong indications of the value of maintaining advertising investment when the economy slows down, together with a number of other insights. My three main conclusions from the research are as follows:

- The most successful companies maximise long-term shareholder value by maintaining their advertising investment when the economy slows down.
- This enables them to build market share at lower cost than when the total market is growing.
- Any reduction in these firms' short-term financial performance is typically soon outweighed by their increased revenue and profit growth when economic conditions improve.

The six readings

The first reading ('Advertising in a recession' by Bernard Ryan Jr) is taken from a monograph published in 1991 by the American Association of Advertising Agencies. It summarises previous research in the US going back to the 1920s, giving the historical background to the other readings.

The next four readings are based on analyses of the PIMS (Profit Impact of Market Strategy) database collected by the Strategic Planning Institute (SPI) in Cambridge, Massachusetts.

Readings 2 ('Advertising during a recession' by Alex Biel and Stephen King) and 3 ('Long-term profitability: advertising versus sales promotion' by Alex Biel) report research in the late 1980s and early 1990s at the Ogilvy Center for Research & Development in San Francisco.

Reading 2 shows that firms which increased Adspend during recessions increased their market share significantly and argues that, in

11

line with other PIMS research, this increase in share is likely to lead to higher profitability (return on investment).

Reading 3 takes this argument further, giving evidence that firms which invested in long-term brand-building (via advertising) were more profitable than those that put most of their marketing budget into promotions.

Readings 4 ('How advertising impacts on profitability' by Leslie Butterfield) and 5 ('Successful competitive strategies for recession and recovery' by Tony Hillier) represent some of the latest PIMS research.

Reading 4 reports that the important links between advertising and long-term profitability (ROI) are through its effects on the perceived quality of the product or service and the firm's general reputation. These – perceived quality and reputation – then drive perceived customer value, which in turn drives market share and profitability.

Further, everything is relative to the competition. What matters is *relative* Adspend (as a proportion of sales, the 'advertising/sales ratio') driving *relative* perceived quality, reputation and customer value. Although this does not fully deal with the question of causality – it partly reflects the fact that high-quality, premium-priced brands tend to spend more on advertising – it does provide some insight into the general mechanisms of longer-term advertising effects.

Reading 5 focuses on the drivers of business performance, specifically during recession and recovery. It concludes that investment in advertising, product innovation and R&D during recession generates high profit during recovery. In contrast, increased fixed capital, working capital, and general/administrative costs, brings no such benefit.

Finally, Reading 6 ('Tough times' by Simon Broadbent) strikes a more cautious note than the other readings. It points out the main limitations of research such as the PIMS studies. First, these studies – by their nature – focus on average effects, while managers deal with specific brands and contexts. Second, the research has not yet sufficiently addressed the issue of causation: if some brands out-advertise and then out-perform other brands, there are likely to be many other differences between the two groups of brands apart from the first group's higher Adspend. Third, and linked to the second, the research has said little about *how and why* advertising might increase long-term profitability: as we have just seen, the latest PIMS studies are starting to address this third criticism.

This does not mean that Simon Broadbent thinks advertisers should automatically cut back when the economy slows down: his criticisms are of the research (including, by implication, the lack of academic research) not the strategy. In fact he stresses several of the positive themes of this book: the value of learning from case histories (like those in Part Two) which give detailed – albeit context-specific – answers to the how and why questions; the need for structured, data-based analysis of longer-term advertising effects and a clear strategy; the option of using recession as an opportunity to strengthen one's market position against weaker rivals ('No more Mr Nice Guy'); and the option of focusing on different segments, benefits, and so on when the economy slows down. In particular, he illustrates the significant benefit (in terms of extra impacts) of advertising when media rates are soft.

Advertising in a Recession

Bernard Ryan Jr

Since the 1920s, US advertising practitioners have done many studies showing that firms that maintain their advertising during recessions tend to gain market share during the recession and increase their profits afterwards. The implication that firms should resist the temptation to cut back advertising when the economy slows down is supported by specific cases.

The best defence is a good offence

The idea of conducting a study to prove that a company should maintain advertising during a recession goes back to the 1920s when an advertising executive named Roland S. Vaile tracked some 200 companies through the recession of 1923. In the April 1927 issue of the Harvard Business Review, he reported that the biggest sales increases throughout the period were rung up by the companies that advertised the most. But Vaile did not take into account such elements as profits or market share. His news fell on deaf ears.

After World War II, Buchen Advertising Inc set out to plot the fortunes of a large number of business-to-business advertisers through successive recessions. In 1947, it began measuring the annual advertising expenditures of each company. It correlated the figures with sales trends before, during, and after the recessions of 1949 and 1954. For the recessions of 1958 and 1961, it also tracked profits. It found not only that sales and profits dropped off, almost without exception, in companies that cut back on advertising. It also revealed that, after the recession had ended, those companies continued to lag behind the ones that had maintained their advertising budgets.

Cahners studies

Several years earlier, the Cahners Publishing Company studied what happened when advertising was cut back in a recession. In 1980, it joined The Strategic Planning Institute (SPI) of Cambridge, Massachusetts, in a major research project. Like the later Centre for Research & Development study, it used SPI's Profit Impact of Market Strategies (PIMS) database, which includes more than 200 corporate members that provide specific information on their nearly 2,000 individual businesses producing industrial products or services. The project evaluated the relationship between brand awareness or preference, market share and profitability, and advertising's impact on this relationship.

In January 1982, Cahners and SPI produced their report, 'Media advertising when your market is in a recession'. It disclosed that *'during a recessionary period, average businesses do experience a slightly lower rate of return relative to normal times. However, expansion times do not generate a higher level of profits than normal periods as might be expected.'* This phenomenon was explained by an analysis of changes in market share. *'During recessionary periods,'* said the Cahners/SPI report, *'these businesses tended to gain a greater share of market. The underlying reason is that competitors, especially smaller marginal ones, are less willing or able to defend against the aggressive firms.'*

The study then pointed out that businesses which increased media advertising expenditures during the recessionary period *'gained an average of 1.5 points of market share'* (Table 1) . Yet, it noted, *'this level of aggressiveness was displayed by only 25 percent of the businesses.'*

TABLE 1: HOW ADVERTISING EXPENDITURES AFFECT SHARE OF MARKET

	Percentage change in advertising expenditure		
	Decrease	**Increase**	
Average point change in share of market conditions		**Up to 28%**	**28–50%**
Recession	0.2	0.5	1.5
Normal	0.2	0.2	0.2
Expansion	−1.0	0.2	0.2

Source: Reprinted by permission of Cahners Publishing Company © 1982

During market expansion periods, on the other hand, some 80% of the businesses increased their media advertising budgets. However, on average, no particular gain in shares was achieved because most of the firms did the same thing.

As for return on investment, the Cahners/SPI study found *'no statistically significant differences in the level of profitability for aggressive media spenders... However, over the long term, increased market share should lead to higher profitability'.*

Conclusion?

A recessionary market condition can provide an opportunity for an industrial business to break from traditional budget-cutting patterns and build a greater share of market through aggressive media advertising. In fact, the study indicated that businesses which are aggressive media spenders can increase their shares of market more than the average business during market downturns. ...Aggressive businesses may be able to accomplish these gains through greater expenditures without reducing short-term profitability[1]

Two other studies: Lestare and General Motors

When Lestare dry bleach and Chicken Sara Lee were being introduced in Fort Wayne, Indiana, the Harvard Business School conducted a study under a grant from the Newsprint Information Committee, which was composed of four Canadian manufacturers of newsprint and supervised by the Bureau of Advertising of the American Newspapers Publishers Association. Advertising for the two new products was limited to the daily News-Sentinel. It agreed to a complex split-run arrangement: in one area of the city, for control purposes, no ads at all would be run for these products; in another area, ads would run once weekly for four weeks and then be dropped; in a third area, ads would run for eight weeks before disappearing; and the fourth section would see 20 weeks of ads. Surveys were conducted among 6,174 women to ascertain brand awareness.

The Lestare results were revealing. Stopping the advertising after four weeks resulted in lower awareness among this subgroup than among the control group that had no advertising exposure whatever, although the brand was in their stores. Among the study's 19 conclusions: *'The consumer's "image" of a product is likely to be more influenced by actual usage than by any amount of advertising exposure. But when advertising stops, awareness of a product "decays".'*

A 1970 strike by the United Auto Workers stopped production of General Motors cars. For 11 weeks, GM's competitors substantially reduced their advertising and other promotional efforts, perhaps under the illusion that they would save their resources for the time when GM was competing again. Professors from the Harvard Business School and the University of Strathclyde in Scotland studied what happened. At that time, the available research indicated that advertising was not a dominant factor among the numerous controllable variables that

1. Dr Valerie Kijewski, 'Media advertising when your market is in a recession', *Cahners Advertising Research Report* No. 2000.7, The Strategic Planning Institute, January 1982.

Advertising during a Recession

Alex Biel and Stephen King

Firms that maintain or increase their advertising during a recession are able to gain market share at a significantly faster rate than when the market is expanding. Although this leads to a reduction in short-term financial performance, the resulting gain in market share should lead to a sustainable increase in the firm's return on investment.

Defining recession

Bernard Baruch said that it's a recession when your neighbour is out of work (adding that when *you're* out of work it's a depression!).

Although the recessions that make the headlines are generally seen as all-encompassing and national in scope, this definition obscures the fact that 'normal' national economic conditions are really an averaging of good times in some industries, bad times in others; growth in some parts of the country and decline in others.

During a national recession everyone gets hurt; but some sectors feel the heat more than others. Conversely, during a period of expansion some markets reap greater benefits.

A more useful, empirically determined definition of recession is one which relates annual growth at one point in time to the longer term growth trend of a *specific market*. The Center for Research & Development, in collaboration with the Strategic Planning Institute, has used this market-specific concept of recession to analyse consumer businesses in the Profit Impact of Market Strategy (PIMS) database. The PIMS database included, at the time of this analysis, 749 consumer businesses, with a minimum of four years' data covering those businesses and the markets in which they participate.[1]

---

1. Since each business unit contributed a minimum of four years of data, and since recessions and expansions were defined as deviations from the normal growth trend of the industry, a given business unit provided at least one, and often more than one observation. Thus the sample of 749 business units provided a total of 1,639 observations.

The PIMS database is the only source that contains both marketing data and financial information for the same consumer-based businesses.

A working definition

For our purposes, a specific market is considered to be in recession when short-term growth *lags* long-term growth by at least four percentage points. On the other hand, when a market *exceeds* its long-term growth rate by more than four percentage points, we can say that it is in a period of expansion.[2] Using this definition, it is possible to describe how consumer businesses fare under different market conditions.

The relationship of changing market conditions

To understand what happens during changing market conditions, it is useful to look at *changes* in rates of return for those businesses enjoying market expansion compared to those suffering a shrinking market. As Figure 1 shows, there is a substantial market effect that impacts a firm's return on invested capital.

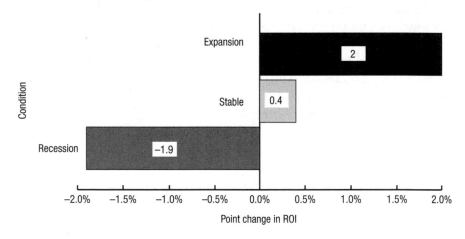

FIGURE 1: CHANGES IN ROI UNDER DIFFERENT MARKET CONDITIONS

It is no great surprise to learn that when the market expands, the average consumer business in the PIMS database enjoys an increased return on investment. Indeed, one might expect rates of return to increase even more sharply during a period of market growth; the fact that they do not

2. For the purposes of this analysis, we define short-term periods as one year. Long-term trends of a market are defined as a minimum of four years.

may be explained to some extent by the difficulty that some businesses face in meeting increased demand.

When a market contracts, on the other hand, the profits of the average business decline. In this study, the average business lost just under two percentage points of profit, dropping from a return on investment of 21.9% to 20.0%.[3]

Changes in advertising spending related to changes in ROI

What is the relationship of changes in advertising spending to changes in return on investment? To answer this question, we looked at the specific spending policies employed by the businesses in the database.

Of the 339 observations of the businesses that experienced recessionary periods, one-third cut their spending on advertising by an average of 11%, while two-thirds actually spent at a *higher* rate than before.[4]

Of those businesses raising their advertising investment, the majority – 60% – limited their increase to no more than 20% more than they had previously been spending. The average business in this group increased spending by 10%. However, the other 40% of those businesses that raised their expenditures made *substantial* increases ranging from 20% to 100%, and averaging 49%.

Table 1 shows how changes in return on investment relate to these changes in spending. Clearly, businesses suffer a reduction in return on investment whether spending is cut or increased during a recession. Indeed, businesses yielding to the natural inclination to cut spending in an effort to increase profits in a recession find that it doesn't work. These businesses fared no better in terms of return on investment than those which modestly increased their ad spending.

TABLE 1: CHANGES IN ROI RELATED TO CHANGES IN ADVERTISING SPENDING DURING A RECESSION

Spending	Changes in ROI
Decreased (ave −11%)	−1.6%
Modest increase (ave +10%)	−1.7%
Substantial increase (ave +49%)	−2.7%
Average change – all businesses (see Figure 1: Recession)	−1.9%

3. Return on investment is calculated before taxes and interest charges for the purpose of this analysis.
4. Some businesses doubtless did take a clearly aggressive stance in light of the softness of the market. But it is probable that for other businesses in the sample spending was committed prior to the receipt of sales or market data. This helps explain why more businesses increased spending than curtailed their efforts.

Those firms that *substantially* increased their advertising budgets experienced the largest drop in return on investment: a reduction of 2.7 percentage points. However, as we shall see, those advertisers who increase spending – whether modestly or aggressively – achieve greater market share gains than those who cut their advertising investment. This, in turn, puts them in a better position to increase profits after the recession.

The links between market conditions, market share, and advertising

These findings led us to dissect the relationship between changes in return on investment and changes in advertising pressure.

As we showed in an earlier study,[5] advertising spending and return on investment are linked – but only indirectly. Advertising directly affects brand 'salience': it makes the advertised brand more top-of-mind among prospects. It also tends to amplify the relative perceived quality of the brand, which in turn increases the brand's perceived value for money. Salience and perceived quality drive buying behaviour, which of course is reflected in sales, and therefore in Share of Market (SOM). But market share is affected by market conditions as well as advertising pressure (Figure 2).

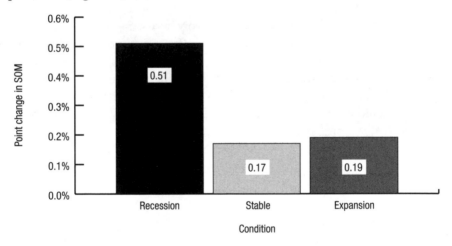

FIGURE 2: CHANGES IN SHARE RELATED TO MARKET CONDITIONS

Here we see that the businesses in the PIMS database enjoy a *higher* rate of share growth during downturns, and a *lower* rate of share increase during stable periods and periods of growth.

5. 'The impact of advertising expenditures on profits for consumer businesses' (The Ogilvy Center for Research & Development, 1987).

One explanation for this is that weaker businesses – businesses with lower market shares – may be less able to defend themselves during downturns, while their larger competitors become more aggressive in order to partially make up sales that are threatened due to a lower growth rate of the total category. The PIMS database includes a broad range of consumer businesses; while some are strong and even market-dominating, others are less successful and weaker. However, on average, the businesses contributing data to PIMS are somewhat more likely to be the stronger players in their markets.[6]

The relationship of advertising spending to market share

To identify the relationship of changes in spending to changes in share of market, we again analysed the data in terms of the spending strategies of the various businesses. As Figure 3 shows, those who reduced their budgets during recession attained much lower share gains than their more aggressive counterparts. On the other hand, marketers which increased spending were able to realise significant market share gains.

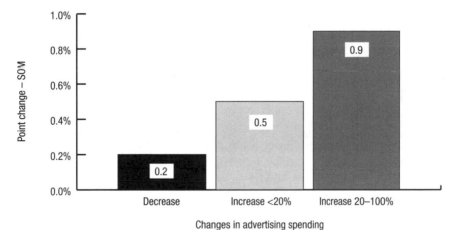

FIGURE 3: CHANGES IN SHARE RELATED TO CHANGES IN ADVERTISING SPENDING DURING RECESSION

It is worth noting that, while there appear to be opportunities to win share by becoming increasingly competitive during a recession, when markets *expand*, share gains are harder to come by. This is demonstrated

6. Since the concept of share of market is a zero sum notion, it is important to note that the share of market averages described here relate to the businesses studied rather than shares of all the entrants in each of the specific markets involved.

in Figure 4, which reveals the link between changing advertising investments and share as markets expand.

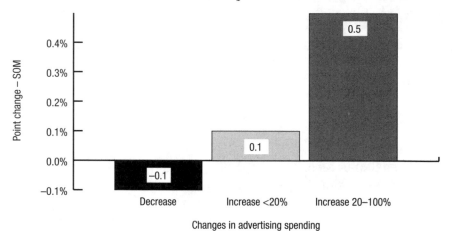

FIGURE 4: CHANGES IN SHARE RELATED TO CHANGES IN ADVERTISING SPENDING DURING EXPANSION

Marketers that decrease their spending during an expansion of the market lose share, albeit slightly; on average, they drop one-tenth of a share point. Those who increase their spending by upwards of 20% as their market expands increase average share, but by only half a percentage point. In other words, *the possibility of gaining share through increasing advertising appears to be greater when the total market is soft.*

It is important to remember that the changes in both share of market and return on investment reported were achieved during the recession itself. Other research indicates that much – but by no means all – of the impact of advertising on sales is achieved in the year the budget is spent.[7] However, the main impact of share gains is translated into gains in profitability in subsequent periods.

While the data reported here are of course correlational, and do not necessarily prove causality, they none the less suggest that there may be some attractive share-building opportunities *during periods when business contracts.* Indeed, the data suggest that aggressive marketers may well find that recessionary periods offer a unique opportunity to build share and position themselves advantageously for the market's recovery.

7. See Reading 3 (Table 2 and Note 2).

The relationship of market share and profitability

In our earlier study of consumer businesses, we found a clear relationship between share of market and return on investment.[8] In fact, this general relationship is not limited to firms marketing to the consumer; it is a robust, well-documented general principle that seems to occur in all markets.

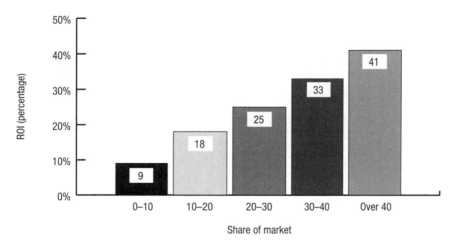

FIGURE 5: MARKET SHARE AND RETURN ON INVESTMENT (ROI)

The specific relationship for the average consumer business is shown in Figure 5. These data suggest that the advertiser who is able to build market share is likely to enjoy a better return on invested capital than is the marketer with a lower market share.

Implications

In general, businesses earn reduced profits when their markets are in recession. But those that cut their advertising expenditures in a recession lose no less in terms of profitability than those who actually increase spending by an average of 10%. In other words, cutting advertising spend to increase short-term profits doesn't seem to work.

More importantly, the data also reveal that a moderate increase in advertising in a soft market can improve share. There is a substantial body of evidence to show that a larger share of the market generally leads to higher return on investment.[9]

8. See Note 5.
9. Robert D. Buzzell and Bradley M. Gale, *The PIMS Principles*, The Free Press, 1987.

For the aggressive marketer, the data suggest that a more ambitious increase in expenditure, although reducing short-term profit, can take advantage of the opportunity afforded by a recession to increase market share even further.

The PIMS data indicate that consumer marketers increasing their spending by an average of 48% during a recession win virtually double the share gains of those who increase their expenditures more modestly. While this aggressive increase in advertising is associated with a drop in return on investment of 2.7% in the short term, it may nevertheless be acceptable to the marketer looking ahead to post-recession growth.

From *Options and Opportunities for Consumer Businesses: Advertising During a Recession*, Alexander L. Biel and Stephen King.

Long-term Profitability: Advertising versus Sales Promotion

Alex Biel

> Packaged-goods firms that put most of their marketing budget into advertising are more profitable (return on investment) than those that put most of their budget into trade and consumer promotions. Advertising works by helping to build strong brands.

This study examines the allocation of funds between advertising and sales promotion. In recent years, marketers have been increasingly turning to sales promotion as a seemingly attractive strategy.

Although many marketers agree that resource allocated to advertising is an investment in long-term brand building, there is far less confidence that advertising is an effective tool in the short or intermediate term. While it is generally accepted that promotions generate short-term sales, some of those sales are simply 'stolen' from future purchases by the same consumer.

I am concerned that this short-term orientation has destructive longer term effects. A major question which marketers must confront is whether excessive emphasis on promotion actually erodes perceived brand value.

If a brand is on 'special' price too frequently, consumers are likely to start to think of the 'special' price as the normal price for the brand – and learn never to buy the brand unless it is discounted. Clearly, we need to pin down the benefits of sales promotion: Does it really build profits for a marketer, as conventional wisdom suggests? Or does it have a negative impact on earnings?

The long-term profit effects of sales promotion

Those questions led to the second collaborative study between the Center for Research & Development and SPI.[1] This time the SPI investigative team was headed by Robert D. Buzzell, Professor of Marketing at Harvard Business School. Again, the PIMS database was used.

For this second study, we further refined the database of 749 consumer businesses to examine businesses with basically similar promotional mechanisms. This led us to examine a group of 314 consumer non-durable businesses – the fast-moving consumer goods (fmcg) businesses included in PIMS, and on which we had both advertising and promotion spending data. Sales promotion, as defined in PIMS, includes both trade and consumer activities (the average US package goods marketer spends 60% of his below-the-line money on trade promotions, and 40% on consumer promotions); most consumer promotions relate to price: temporary cut-price offers, premiums, direct couponing and money-back deals. Contests, games and sweepstakes are also included in this category.

To examine the relationship between various strategies on the one hand and payout on the other, the sample of business units was divided into three approximately equal parts, based on a frequency distribution of their allocation patterns:

– businesses using sales promotion as their dominant strategy,
– businesses using a mixed strategy,
– businesses using advertising as their major marketing investment vehicle.

Businesses using promotion as the dominant strategy were defined as all businesses spending less than 36% of their marketing funds in advertising. The average business in this group spent only 23% of their marketing money on advertising and 77% on sales promotion.

The group using the 'mixed strategy' actually skewed slightly towards promotions. This segment of PIMS fmcg businesses spent between 36% and 50% of their marketing money on advertising. On average, they placed about 44% of their marketing expenditures in advertising, and 56% in promotions.

The final group comprised that set of businesses which used advertising as their dominant spending strategy. To be included in this group, businesses had to place over 50% of marketing investment in

1. 'Advertising, sales promotion and the bottom line' (The Ogilvy Center for Research and Development, 1989).

advertising. The average business in this group allocated two-thirds of its marketing funds to media advertising, and the rest to promotion. Table 1 gives the performance of each group.

TABLE 1: RELATIONSHIP OF ADVERTISING/PROMOTION MIX TO RETURN ON INVESTMENT

Advertising/promotion mix	Average ROI (%)
Advertising emphasis	30
Mixed strategy	22
Promotion emphasis	18

Those companies spending the bulk of their funds – 76% – on promotion, achieved an average return of 18.1% (pre-tax and pre-interest charges).

Those employing the mixed strategy, where on average 44% went to advertising and 56% went to promotions, earned a considerably more respectable average return on investment of 27.3%.

The group of marketers using advertising as their dominant strategy – that is, businesses investing more than 50% of their marketing resources in advertising – registered the healthiest return on investments of all, averaging 30.5%.

The other measures of performance included in the analysis, such as return on sales and share of market, all showed similar patterns; but as might be expected, the magnitude of the differences varied. It is clear that there is a positive relationship between the emphasis on investment in advertising and profitability. Conversely, those businesses that allocate most of their marketing budgets to promotion tend to have lower profit margins and rates of return on investment.

The effect of extra ad expenditure

One final piece of evidence comes from another source. These other data were developed by Information Resources Incorporated, a leading US research firm. They studied the impact of extra advertising spending on sales for 15 fmcg brands in a highly controlled experiment. The average brand they studied increased its advertising spending by 70% during the one-year test.[2]

2. Magid Abraham, 'Fact base design to improve advertising and promotion productivity', Proceedings, 2nd Annual ARF Advertising and Promotion Workshop, 1990.

The IRI measurement system, 'BehaviorScan', is state-of-the-art, and quite high tech. It controls the advertising reaching test homes and measures what members of these households purchase through scanners at the checkout counters of stores in the market. This makes it possible to compare households receiving the extra advertising with a matched control group receiving only the normal advertising spend.

As Table 2 shows, the average increase in sales among those receiving the additional advertising pressure during the year of the test was 22%. Not bad, but the story does not end there.

TABLE 2: ADVERTISING-INDUCED SALES INCREASE FOR THREE YEARS

Year	Average sales increase (%)
Test year	22
1st post-test year	17
2nd post-test year	6
Cumulative total	**45**

At the end of the one-year test, the extra advertising completely stopped. Both groups of households – the test group that had previously received the higher level of advertising, and the control group – received exactly the same level of advertising pressure over the next year for the test brands.

One year after the test, there continued to be higher sales among those households which had received the heavier advertising weight. These on average bought 17% more than those receiving the base level advertising. In year three – two years after the heavy spending test – those who had received the higher weight during the test continued to purchase 6% more of the average test brand than those in the control group. So it seems that additional advertising pressure has an enduring effect in addition to its immediate effect.

In another analysis of the profitability of more than 60 trade promotions using the same technology for data collection, IRI found that overall only 16% of the promotions paid out. In addition, for established brands, the long-term effects were likely to be negative due to stockpiling by loyal buyers on the one hand and 'training' buyers to wait for deals on the other.

Conclusions

I will summarise what these various PIMS and IRI studies are telling us.

First, when we look at advertising alone, it makes a measurable direct contribution to perceived quality, and share of market, which leads to profitability.

Second, advertising appears to have a carry-over sales effect that extends beyond the period during which it is actually running.

Third, when we separately examine the way in which businesses allocate their expenditures to sales promotion and to advertising, we see that those businesses emphasising advertising enjoy a higher return on invested capital.

Finally, we see a significant relationship between changes in market share and changes in advertising spending, but not between share changes and promotional changes. Clearly, money invested in advertising not only drives profits on a yearly basis, but also builds strong brands.

Design, packaging, public relations, sales promotion, experience with the brand and word-of-mouth all contribute to – or, in some cases, detract from – these values. But advertising has traditionally played the leading role in shaping and defining the image of strong brands.

In this reading I have presented evidence from PIMS showing that advertising makes a measurable, significant contribution to brand profitability. It does this in the year in which the advertising budget is spent, so there is an attractive *short-term* payout.

Data from IRI were also presented, however, illustrating that the carry-over effect of advertising continues to produce higher sales in the years immediately following the expenditure: a longer term payout, and a welcome additional benefit.

Advertising produces these results by adding value to products and services. It produces these results by turning products and services into strong brands that have more leverage with middlemen; brands that can credibly pre-empt the truth; brands that enjoy higher loyalty; brands that are more forgiving of owners who occasionally stumble; brands that command better margins and are more resistant to price competition; brands that can be extended.

Advertising builds brands that mean more to the consumer. These brands can, in principle, live forever. In other words, advertising works by building strong brands.

From 'Strong brand, high spend. tracking relationships between the marketing mix and brand values', Alexander L. Biel, *Admap*, November 1990.
© NTC Publications Ltd, 1990

How Advertising Impacts on Profitability

Leslie Butterfield

Relative advertising expenditure (advertising/sales ratio relative to competitors) helps to build (i) the relative perceived quality of the product or service and (ii) the firm's relative reputation. These, in turn, help to build relative perceived customer value, which is the main driver of market share and long-term profitability.

Tom Peters, the celebrated management consultant, describes PIMS as being 'the world's most extensive strategic information database'. From its genesis at Harvard in 1972, it now encompasses data on over 3,000 companies – totalling a massive 20,000 years of business experience! Suffice to say here that the focus for this study was the 200+ companies operating principally in branded consumer products in Europe (see Figure 1).

The IPA's interest in the PIMS database stems from an awareness of the growing demand from senior management for 'general proofs' of the value of advertising, perhaps to set alongside the expanding databank of individual case studies of advertising effectiveness that the IPA has assembled over the last 18 years.

Among these general proofs are the long-term studies conducted by, among others, AC Nielsen on the negative effect on brand share of the removal of advertising support, work in the US by the American Association of Advertising Agencies on the impact of advertising on stock price performance, and work by a number of academics over the past two recessions to identify the long-term effects of significant decreases in promotional support for brands.

In addition to these, the IPA has been active in promoting the issue of brand valuation – as a means by which marketing companies and their agencies can understand better the considerable intangible value of their branded assets – and invest in them accordingly.

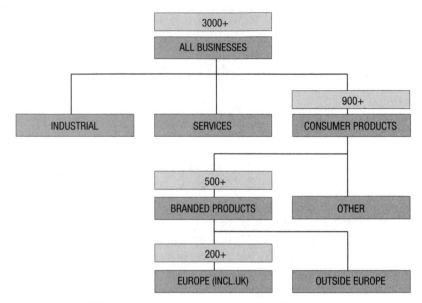

FIGURE 1: SELECTING COMPARISONS FROM THE PIMS DATABASE
Source: PIMS Database © 1998 PIMS Europe Ltd

The analysis described here, by contrast, focuses specifically on the relationship between advertising and profitability[1] – both directly and, perhaps more importantly, indirectly via the medium of perceived quality.

The importance of perceived quality to brand buying decisions and loyalty is hard to overstate. David Aaker in his excellent book *Building Successful Brands* describes the power of the relationship fully, and concludes:

Perceived quality is the single most important contributor to a company's return on investment (ROI), having more impact than market share, R&D or marketing expenditures... [it] is usually at the heart of what customers are buying, and in that sense, it is a bottom-line measure of the impact of a brand identity. More interesting, though, perceived quality reflects a measure of 'goodness' that spreads over all elements of the brand.... When perceived quality improves, so generally do other elements of customers' perception of the brand.

Our quest here therefore was to explore the quantitative *and* causal relationship between advertising, perceived quality and profitability. Like most quests, ours was not a simple journey.

---

1. Defined for the purposes of this paper as return on investment (ROI).
From 'How advertising impacts on profitability', Leslie Butterfield, *AdValue*, Issue 1, September 1998.

The PIMS model

Figure 2 illustrates the well-established causal relationships that we know to exist within the main PIMS database.

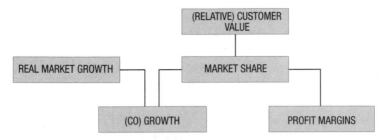

FIGURE 2: LINKS FROM CUSTOMER VALUE TO PROFITABILITY AND GROWTH
Source: PIMS Database © 1998 PIMS Europe Ltd

PIMS are unequivocal that, on the basis of the whole sample of 3,000+ businesses, providing a superior value offering to customers (whether that be trade customers or consumers of branded products) is a prime driver of growth and profitability.

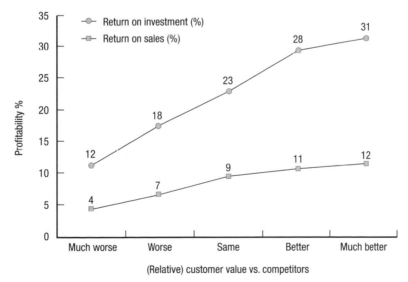

FIGURE 3: CUSTOMER VALUE DRIVES PROFITABILITY
Source: PIMS Database © 1998 PIMS Europe Ltd

Furthermore, within our subsample of branded consumer products, we can show that relative customer value is highly correlated with profitability (see Figure 3). Customer value in turn is defined from the customer's perspective as a combination of quality of total offering and price, both of these being measured relative to competitors.

Of these two, given the strength of David Aaker's argument above, (and indeed from PIMS' own evidence), it is relative perceived quality that is of most interest to us.

Hence our need for an analysis that would allow us to examine the direct and causal relationship between advertising and profitability via the intermediate variable of relative perceived quality.

Finally, we also knew that one of the principal components of relative quality is 'product image and company reputation' (see Figure 4). Armed with these numerous linkages and relationships, we went on to examine the extent to which we could demonstrate the role that advertising spend can play in shaping and influencing these factors.

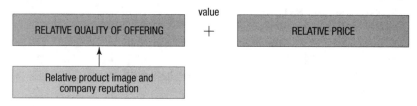

FIGURE 4: THE KEY COMPONENTS OF CUSTOMER VALUE

PIMS special analysis

Our first special analysis was designed to examine the relationship between absolute levels of advertising spend (expressed as a percentage of sales) and relative quality of offering. The findings are shown in Figure 5.

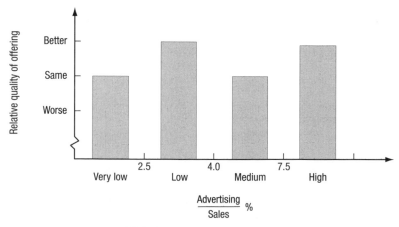

FIGURE 5: ABSOLUTE LEVELS OF ADVERTISING SPEND ARE NOT STRONGLY CORRELATED WITH RELATIVE QUALITY OF OFFERING

Superficially, the results appear disappointing: there is little correlation between absolute levels of advertising spend and relative quality of offering.

Spirits rose considerably though when we repeated the analysis, but this time looking at advertising spend (again expressed in A:S terms) relative to competitors... effectively a measure of 'share of voice' relative to share of market. Figure 6 shows the findings from this analysis and the result is clear: advertising spend *relative to competitors* is strongly correlated with relative quality of offering.

The conclusion here is clear and important. Namely, that in influencing customers' perceptions of the quality of your product (and hence its value) it is not a question of how *much* you spend, but of how much you _out_spend your competitors.

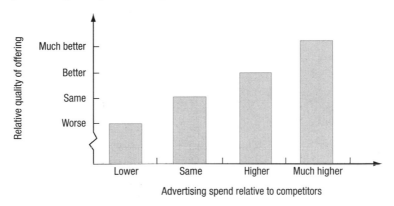

Advertising spend relative to competitors

FIGURE 6: ADVERTISING SPEND RELATIVE TO COMPETITORS IS STRONGLY CORRELATED WITH RELATIVE QUALITY OF OFFERING

Two further points are worth noting here:

1. Because there is no correlation in the analysis at Figure 5, paradoxically this gives us *more* confidence in the causality of the relationship described in Figure 6. If the reverse causality were true, ie that better quality led to higher adspend, we would expect the same relationship to be reflected in the absolute spends in Figure 5 as in the relative spends at Figure 6. As this is not the case, our confidence in the *true* causality of Figure 6 increases.
2. The point about outspending competitors should not be taken as a 'counsel of despair' by No. 2 brands and below. What we are saying here is that those brands need to outspend (in share of voice terms) *relative to their share of market* – not absolutely more than, for example the brand leader. This same logic held

true when we went on to examine a key component of perceived quality: product image and company reputation. Again the analysis showed little evidence of correlation between *absolute* spends and this component. But when we examined our *relative* spend measure (ie share of voice) the correlation was powerful (see Figure 7).

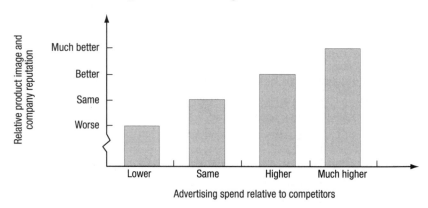

FIGURE 7: ADVERTISING SPEND RELATIVE TO COMPETITORS IS ALSO STRONGLY CORRELATED WITH RELATIVE PRODUCT IMAGE AND COMPANY REPUTATION

It is this analysis that leads to our second key conclusion from this study.

Because 'product image and company reputation' is both a component of quality and *a driver of it*, we would suggest that it is not just 'any old advertising' that matters, but rather advertising that seeks and succeeds in building quality perceptions of the product, either directly or through the intermediary of product image and company reputation.

The combination of these two special analyses, and the conclusions that stem from them, mean that we can now extend the model that we first examined in Figure 2. Figure 8 shows that extended model – with the top three levels having been added as a result of the analyses reported here. Furthermore, we can be fairly confident about the causality (and not just the correlation) of each of the individual linkages illustrated.

Conclusions

While it would be delightful to have been able to show a direct causal relationship between advertising and profitability, the real world influence of other factors means that we have had to demonstrate causality through a set of intervening variables.

40

Of these, by far the most important is relative customer value – and we are able to demonstrate the impact of advertising on this variable, through its effect on relative perceived quality.

Importantly, however, we have seen that it is relative (rather than absolute) advertising spend levels that show a strong correlation here. This leads to the interesting conclusion that it is not how much you spend, but how much you outspend competitors that matters.

The data also suggest a second conclusion: that the *nature* of the advertising matters too – its focus should be on product image, company reputation and/or other key attributes that drive customers' perceptions of relative quality and hence value.

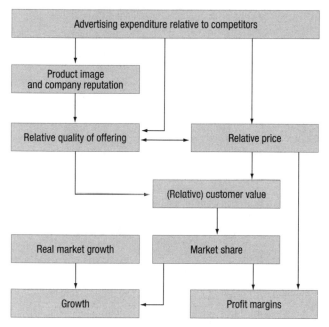

FIGURE 8: LINKS FROM ADVERTISING TO PROFITABILITY AND GROWTH

The linkages thus arrived at (summarised in Figure 8) are more complex than we might have wished for in an ideal world – but they do at least have a 'real world' feel to them.

The analysis described here does not suggest that *all* advertising leads to increased profitability (ie that there is a universal relationship here); but it does strongly suggest that advertising which builds quality does have just that effect.

Rarely are causal relationships easy to demonstrate in areas such as advertising. At least, with this analysis, we can have confidence in the ultimate effect of advertising on corporate fortunes. And while the linkages we have been able to demonstrate are less simple than most models of advertising effect, they may be more honest than some.

© Institute of Practitioners in Advertising, 1998

Successful Competitive Strategies for Recession and Recovery: Evidence from PIMS

Tony Hillier

Investment in marketing, product innovation and R&D during a recession sets the platform for strong performance during the recovery. In contrast, investment in fixed capital, working capital, and general and administrative costs does not. However, market leaders can lose out on recovery if they chop too much capacity in the recession.

'To boldly go...' is the clear message from new research we have undertaken into which business strategies aid success through a recession. For strong businesses, bold strategies are the way to continue thriving, and for weak businesses they are the routes to survival. The new study, based on the PIMS (Profit Impact of Market Strategy) database of business performance, points to very clear strategies for securing the future both during and after a recession – in other words, how to maintain profitability through the bad times and achieve superior sustainable growth during recovery.

The evidence is drawn from a sample of nearly 1,000 businesses in the PIMS database of business performance (see Appendix at the end of this Reading), which have all experienced recession and recovery. A market in 'recession' is defined as experiencing two years' decline in volume followed by two years of growth. Importantly, this definition necessarily excludes markets that are in terminal decline. Also note that we are identifying total markets that experienced decline and recovery in volume demand. This does not necessarily mean that the sales volume of a single, successful business fell – only that the total market demand for its type of products/services declined and then grew again.

In this research we have highlighted three measures to distinguish between successful and unsuccessful strategies for the 1,000 businesses (Figure 1).

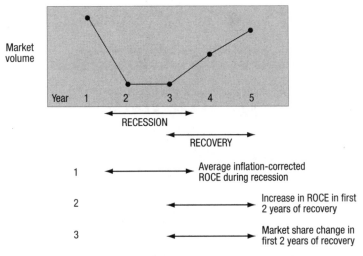

FIGURE 1: THREE MEASURES FOR PERFORMANCE DURING RECESSION AND RECOVERY

Successful strategies: increased investment in marketing

First let us look at what have proved to be 'good costs' – those which should, if anything, be increased during recession. The most pointed of these findings is the importance of marketing. The natural reaction of many businesses experiencing a downturn is to cut costs in areas like advertising and promotion. Our findings prove that they should do exactly the opposite if they are to ride out the recession and thrive thereafter.

We divided the 1,000 PIMS businesses between those that cut, maintained and increased marketing spend during recession. As Figure 2 shows, those businesses that increased marketing spend were not significantly less profitable during recession. However, their profits increased dramatically faster once recovery started, unlike 'cutters' of marketing spend whose profitability actually fell when recovery began. Furthermore, businesses which increased marketing spend in recession gained market share three times as fast as 'cutters' once recovery began (Figure 2).

For marketing spend to be effective, of course, it needs to be based on a sound customer proposition. Those businesses which, *in their customers' eyes,* provide better value for money than their competitors are both more profitable during recession and grow faster once recovery starts (Figure 3).[1]

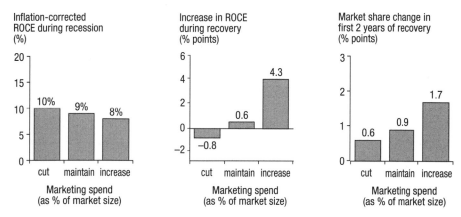

FIGURE 2: MARKETING SPEND DOES NOT DAMAGE ROCE SIGNIFICANTLY IN A RECESSION AND HELPS SET THE PLATFORM FOR STRONG RECOVERY

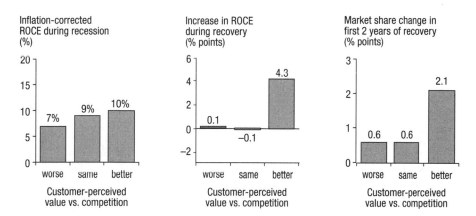

FIGURE 3: SUPERIOR VALUE FOR MONEY PAYS OFF THROUGH A RECESSION (AS ALWAYS)

Improving the perceived quality of your offering relative to competitors during recession also pays off in better profits and growth (Figure 4).

---

1. See also the June 1998 issue of Marketing Business for PIMS' general findings about the profit impact of superior value for money for customers.

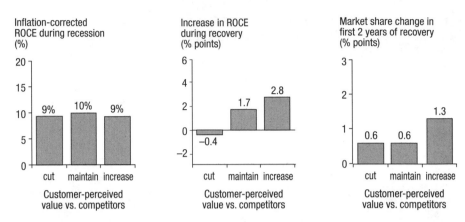

FIGURE 4: MOVING AHEAD OF COMPETITORS ON CUSTOMER-PERCEIVED QUALITY PAYS OFF HANDSOMELY THROUGH INTO A RECOVERY

Successful strategies: product innovation and R&D

What about product innovation and R&D during recession? Both pay off handsomely (Figures 5 and 6).

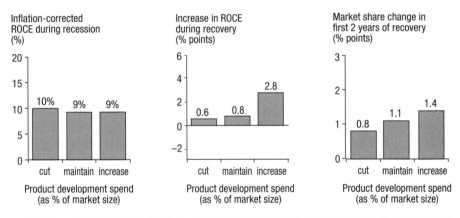

FIGURE 5: RECESSIONS ARE A GOOD TIME FOR PRODUCT R&D INITIATIVES

Why should R&D spend be such a particularly 'good cost' during recession? Because successful, new product introductions during recession are crucial to strong recovery in profitability and growth (Figure 7).

A good example of a successful business launching new products during a recession is Gillette's 1990 launch of its Gillette Sensor brand of shaving products. Since the launch of Gillette Sensor products, more than 8 billion Sensor razor blade cartridges and 400 million Sensor razors have been sold!

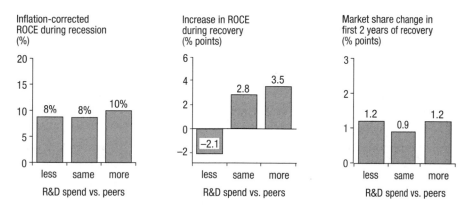

FIGURE 6: R&D APPEARS TO BE A PARTICULARLY 'GOOD COST' IN A RECESSION

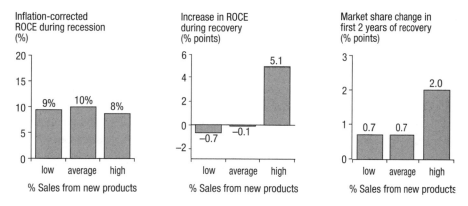

FIGURE 7: NEW PRODUCTS ARE CRUCIAL TO PROFIT RECOVERY

Not so good: investment in fixed assets

Let's turn now to 'bad costs'. Investing in new fixed assets during recession, supposedly to improve cost competitiveness and productivity, does not usually bring positive benefits and, if anything, the opposite is the case. Why should this be? Because the supposed benefits of new assets tend to get competed away in the form of lower prices and profit margins in an attempt to fill capacity (Figure 8).

Other 'bad costs' include high working capital, high manufacturing costs and high administrative overheads.

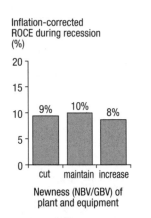
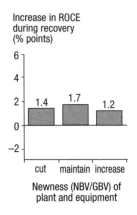
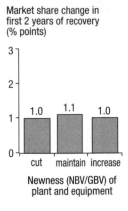

FIGURE 8: NEW PLANT AND EQUIPMENT (WHICH EATS UP CASH) HAS NO DISCERNIBLE POSITIVE EFFECTS ON RESULTS ... IF ANYTHING, THE OPPOSITE
Source: PMS Database, 1998 PIMS Europe Ltd

Understanding when 'it depends'

There are certain strategies that do not always contribute only positively or negatively to business performance. This is because their impact depends on the strategic position of the business. These strategies include output capacity and out-sourcing.

Cutting output capacity during recession (and, thus, people and costs) may seem an appropriate strategy. For market leaders, however, the PIMS evidence suggests that cutting capacity holds back profit and share improvement during recovery (Figure 9, market leaders only).

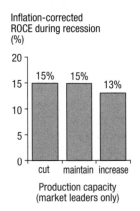
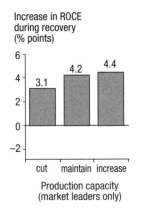
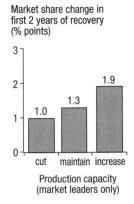

FIGURE 9: MARKET LEADERS CAN LOSE OUT ON RECOVERY IF THEY CHOP TOO MUCH CAPACITY IN THE RECESSION

Next we have the issue of out-sourcing. This is a rapidly increasing trend, partly to enable businesses to concentrate on their core competencies and partly to realise supposed cost savings and efficiencies. So, what better time to out-source more of your services than in a recession? The PIMS evidence suggests that 'it depends' on your market position and whether your priority for recovery is profit or share improvement (Figure 10).

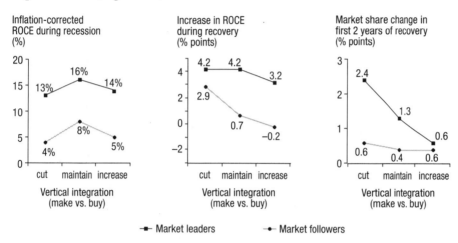

FIGURE 10: OUT-SOURCING DEPENDS ON MARKET POSITIONS AND RECOVERY STRATEGY

In conclusion, have bold strategies ...

The PIMS evidence suggests that during a recession there are some costs where the optimum stays steady or even increases ('good costs') and other costs where the optimum drops dramatically ('bad costs'). 'Optimum' relates both to performance through the recession and to the recovery thereafter.

'Good costs in recession'	'Bad costs in recession'	Depends on strategic strength
• Marketing	• Fixed capital	• Retaining spare capacity
• Quality	• Working capital	• Price aggression
• Product development	• General and administration	• Out-sourcing

... but beware the panacea

The evidence reported here provides a guide for which strategies should prove successful during recession for many businesses much of the time. They are *not* a panacea for all businesses in all circumstances. Indeed, for certain businesses, opposite 'rules' seem to apply. For example, we evaluated one type of business with a particular set of strategic characteristics where a successful strategy in recession was to cut back on product launches and to increase investment in overheads in order to improve the quality of interaction with customers and suppliers.

The best way to ensure that you adopt the right strategies in recession for your businesses is to determine which strategies have proved successful for businesses analogous to your own.

Appendix: The PIMS database in 1998

At the end of 1998, the PIMS Database encompassed approximately 3,500 businesses from a wide range of industries in North America, Europe and other parts of the world.

- average profitability during recession, defined as return on capital employed (ROCE);
- change in profitability (ROCE) during first two years of recovery;
- change in market share during first two years of recovery.

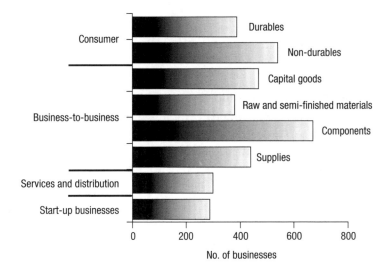

PIMS data on each of these businesses capture over 200 characteristics about the markets they serve, their market shares and the shares of their main competitors, the resources required by the businesses, their costs and financial performance. For each of these businesses, at least four consecutive years of data are compiled.

Successful Competitive Strategies for Recession and Recovery

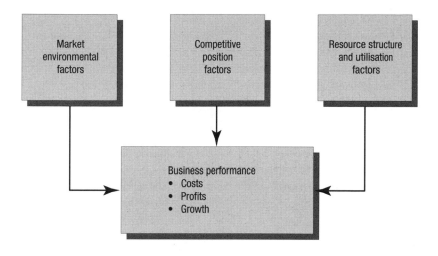

From 'Successful competitive strategies for recession and recovery', Tony Hillier, Market Leader, Spring 1999.
© NTC Publications Ltd, 1999

READING 6

Tough Times

Simon Broadbent

Detailed analytical case studies (like those in Part Two) are more persuasive arguments for maintaining or increasing advertising spend during recessions, than testimonials and statistical studies which suggest that firms should maintain or increase advertising during recessions without saying how or why. Advertisers should also explore the longer-term benefits of advertising their specific brands, as well as looking for opportunities: to emphasise different customer segments or benefits when the economy slows down; to capture market share aggressively from weaker rivals; and to exploit the opportunities created by softer media rates.

I have read many papers of advice given to advertisers on how to cope in tough times. As I read, my usual reaction is scepticism – at various levels. I suspect that some advertisers feel the same. This is therefore a Devil's Advocate approach, intended to help the industry by seeing how our defence can be improved.

I have put the papers into six groups, of increasing persuasiveness or usefulness. At the end I offer a suggestion for a different way of approaching the opportunity.

1 Testimonials

At the extreme is the lucky lottery winner argument:

> *'We've weathered several periods when times weren't so good, and so I don't think we'll cancel our advertising now. In fact, we might even increase it.'*
>
> (W.K. Kellogg, 1929)

> *'We see this as a time to strengthen the brand image of Toyota... we have posted a healthy increase in fourth quarter spending.'*
>
> (Head of Marketing, Toyota, 1990)

Personally, when I see the smiling faces of lottery winners, I experience no increased conviction that I should rush out and buy tickets. In the same way, my reaction to this sort of argument is to ask whether breakfast products might be a recession-proof category, and to wonder whether Toyota were on a roll in the 1990s anyway. I feel, very sceptically, that things may not be the same for me and for my products. Do you think that your own odds have improved when you hear about individual successes?

2 Average expectations

At the next level we are presented with averages, rather than isolated examples. For instance, Alexander Biel[1] has carried out a relevant analysis of the PIMS database. He found 339 strategic business units that went through a period of shrinking markets. These were at different times – he is not dealing with a general regression. He divided them approximately into thirds by the way their advertising budgets compared with the previous year, and then looked at overall return on investment (ROI) (Table 1).

TABLE 1

Advertising	Percent change in ROI
Reduced	−1.6
Increase averaged 10%	−1.7
Increase averaged 50%	−2.7

This is a sobering table: in tough times the average business sees its return on investment fall. Not a surprise. But those who invest in more advertising do not see an immediate or increasing return. So why do they do it? See Table 2.

1. A.L. Biel (1998) "Reduced advertising and its impact on profitability and market share in a recession, pp 297–307 in *How Advertising Works*, John Philip Jones (Ed.), Sage Publications. Note that at the AA meeting this source was criticised, and it certainly seems inconsistent with the more recent analyses. The detail is not as important as the sort of argument used. [NB: Reading 2 by Biel and King is based on the same study. Ed.]

TABLE 2

Advertising	Share of market points increase
Reduced	0.2
Increase averaged 10%	0.5
Increase averaged 50%	0.9

Those who advertised generally increased market share, and it was on average proportional to the amount by which advertising changed.

This is more persuasive. It makes a general case. But there are two problems.

First, how much variation was there within these groups? Were there some negative examples? I don't manage an average brand, so why should I rely on the average?

Second, the reader is invited to read the table like an experiment and to conclude, 'If I reduce advertising, this… if I increase it, that…'. But it may not be reporting an experiment in which advertising was the only factor. Suppose, for example, those who increased advertising did so because they had an innovation to announce. The synergy of advertising and innovation gets market share increase. But if I do not have an innovation, I cannot expect changing an ad decision to have this sort of effect.

3 Role models

At a higher level are individual case histories, where I am given enough information to judge whether the conditions facing the manufacturer may apply to me. It is more work to study many individual examples, but increasing relevance in this way can be worthwhile.

My scepticism is most likely to melt when I learn that someone close to my situation has benefited from investment – because I also learn *how* and *why*. It is lessons from my own category that I find most persuasive.

4 Self-examination

I get more assistance when the adviser asks me the questions I need to face up to. I do not now just look at the experience of others but am helped to use my own information to decide on my own action. Such is the help given in a recent US publication.[2] For example, this reports a

2. 'The next recession – strategies to help your company cope and compete' (Leo Burnett Public Relations, Chicago, 1998).

survey which was used to segment consumers into four types:

- – The recession-proof
- – The solution-seeker
- – The security-seeker
- – The vulnerable.

It is useful to know where your consumers stand in tough times, and hence, for a multi-product company, which of your brands it is best to support.

Similarly, I have seen lists of categories known to resist hard times, while others (who probably know who they are!) are right to take more extreme action. Just like brands, categories are all different and generalisations aren't that much help.

There is further advice about scenario construction, to help prepare yourself in a relevant way; you should reassure your stakeholders that you are taking appropriate action, and so on. I find this a practical and worthwhile approach. Thus too, 'Advertising can skilfully reposition a product to take advantage of new buying concerns, or give an advertiser a stable image in a chaotic environment.'[3]

Examples[4] are: '*A-1 Steak Sauce isn't just for sirloin any more – commercials show people pouring A-1 on "recession-staple" hamburgers;*' or, '*Ziploc food bags boast their airtight seal, but the emphasis becomes that left-overs need special treatment.*'

There are lessons here for both planners and creatives. Match the current mood, emphasise risk-avoidance if this hits the spot, show what pleasures are affordable. Another piece of advice, which struck a chord with me, was that media buyers should now negotiate long-term deals that will be advantageous later when prices rise again.

If only… .

Of course none of these roundabout defences of communication would be necessary if we had a direct method. If only we could calculate, even roughly, what the benefits of maintaining or increasing Adspend really are in our own case, with a particular campaign. Then we could move into justification for spending in a recession with an argument that a sceptical finance director just has to agree with.

I now give three lines of thought which attempt to provide such an argument. They try to meet the objections I raised above to some of the more common approaches. Their aim is to lay down a theoretical

---

3. *Case for Advertising in a Recession* (American Business Press).
4. 'Advertising during a recession', Direct Marketing (1991), 54(5), p 17.

foundation. Thus they may explain *why* we might believe the weaker arguments.

5 Long-term benefits

First would be a direct calculation of the long-term benefits of advertising.

Unfortunately there is no agreed way to carry out such a calculation. It is in my view the most important task facing advertising researchers – to quantify, in an individual case, the long-term benefits of advertising. We really need to work harder on this at all times, not just in hard times.

This need is widely recognised. The IPA ad effectiveness competition is broadening in exactly this direction. Methods do of course exist, and evidence has been published, that direct effects on sales can continue long after the limits normally used for 'short-term effects' have been passed. Even short-term effects are certainly longer than the single week claimed by one or two researchers and currently used in the US by several schedulers.

Reviewing the work of Andrew Roberts and Walter Reichel on single-source data, and of the many analysts who use time-series data, plus my own experience, has convinced me that half-lives of two, three and perhaps up to six weeks are the norm for short-term effects.[5]

Such effects are no argument for investing now in order to reap benefits in a year or two. They also hardly represent the general conviction that traces from advertising can last for years. Nor do they justify the ad investment itself in the short term, in most cases.

The famous IRI summary[6] of 44 tests is worth recalling. This showed that after a year of upweights which gave on average a +22% sales increase, the next year without an upweight produced +14% and the third year still had +7%.

Many case histories have been published about long-term adstock modelling and other inspections of the base above which the short-term effects operate. These have come particularly from Millward Brown both in the UK and the US, but also from others, including work by Tim Fry and myself. I regretfully cannot call on any of them as firm and certain grounds for calculation in every case.

5. The estimates have decreased as shorter time intervals are used to make them. Weekly data give different estimates from four-weekly or monthly data, let alone bi-months. We are only beginning to understand this so-called interval effect. See T. Fry, S. Broadbent and J. Dixon, 'Estimating half life and the interval bias', submitted to the *International Journal of Research in Marketing*.
6. L.M. Lodish and B. Lubetkin (1992) 'General truths? nine key findings from IRI test data', *Admap*, February, pp 9–15.

6 No more Mr Nice Guy

Up to this point, the arguments have been rather gentlemanly. The brand has been seen as landscape, the variants are fields which are tilled and fertilised – and then bring forth their harvest.

In the real world, the scene is not pastoral and the brand is not alone. It is more of an animal, fighting in a Darwinian jungle for survival against competitors. If it were a game, it's certainly a zero-sum game. My gain has to be your loss. It is more relevant to monitor share in tough times than volume.

Being Mr Nice Guy in such a world is a big mistake. Finishing last is not an option in hard times. It is therefore essential to decide how tough you can be. Can your resources out-punch your opponent? Can you count on the determination of your CEO and your finance committee? Is your company capable of delivering the death blow? Can it 'think murderous', as *Fortune* put it? Does it see a recession as a wonderful time to have an unfair advantage?

If your company is well funded and confident, then a simple argument applies. In tough times, everyone loses (the PIMS example showed that) – but not in proportion to size. Suppose my opponent weighs in at 100, but I'm at 120 – a 20% advantage. Then comes the downturn and knocks 20 off everyone. I may be down to 100, but my opponent is now at 80 – and I have an increased advantage, at 25%. This is the opportunity for aggression.

More directly, the message is that the strong become relatively stronger – and this is the time to use your strength. The argument is not helpful to the weak, to those with only a short-term horizon, to those who are afraid of risk. No wonder tough times are referred to as a shake-out.

When Leo Burnett founded his agency in the middle of the Great Depression he may have had two advantages – the first is less competition. The second is counter-intuitive, but makes sense: a market needs strengthening precisely when it is weak. The very fact of starting an agency was an act of courage and encouraged like-minded people. In a services business, this leads to bonding.

7 Long-term scheduling

My last argument follows from some work I have been doing recently on *when* to advertise:[7] the scheduling problem, or how to spread your TV budget over the year.

7. Admap Publications plan to release my book with this title in September 1999.

But why take a year as the limit? What happens if we look at a longer period, say, one which includes a general downturn in the economy?

The process I recommend for normal scheduling starts with an evaluation of the *value* to you of persuading shoppers, over the weeks of the year you are planning. For example, the seasonality of volume sales in your category might give a guide. Then, what do you expect to have to pay for TV time each week? *Costs* actually vary across the year in quite a systematic way, so both of these numbers are quite easy to forecast.

A useful index, showing when you might well concentrate your efforts, is *value/cost* – when this is high, it's a good time to choose. This is the first step in scheduling.

What happens when we apply this idea to several years?

I take annual UK data between 1986 and 1997, and start with the amount which consumers spent in real terms in three selected categories. Figure 1 shows that 1990–92 were indeed low years – food did not recover until 1995. The drops were however remarkably small – we are talking only a few percentage points.

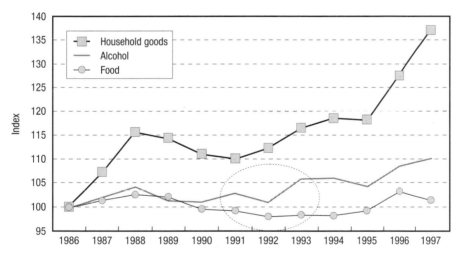

FIGURE 1: CONSUMER SPEND, 1997 PRICES, INDEXED ON 1986

How did advertisers react to these small changes? We all know advertising is subject to a multiplier and Figure 2 shows how large this is. We are now talking tens of percentage points. The reasons for this are panic and the raiding of the ad budget.

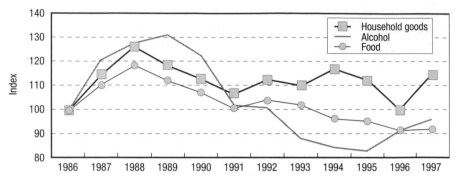

FIGURE 2: REGISTER – MEAL TOTAL SPEND, 1990 PRICES, INDEXED ON 1986

What effect did this have on costs? Figure 3 shows how the TV index swings by amounts between the first two charts – by a lot more than consumers' spend, but not as much as the drop in TV revenue (you may well ask why). The Advertising Association says the press data here is not very reliable, but the TV data are pretty firm.

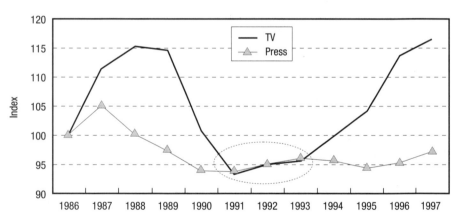

FIGURE 3: TV AND PRESS COSTS, INDEXED ON 1986

I now take the TV costs, and divide them into the consumer spends. This gives value/cost: when it is high, it's a good time to spend. The peaks in Figure 4 are in 1991 and 1993. Note incidentally that value/cost has fallen for food and drink every year since 1993.

Clearly the years 1991–93 were a bargain – up to 10% or even 15% a better buy than at the end of this period. If these were monthly figures, with such peaks in value/cost, buyers would be scrambling over each other to get into them. Instead, due to pressures we all understand, advertisers reacted as we saw in Figure 2. 'Understand', I say, not 'sympathise'.

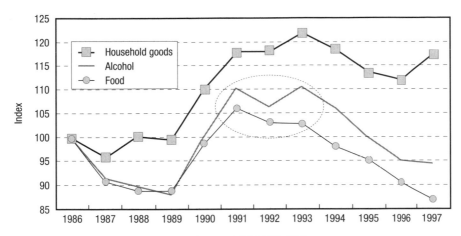

FIGURE 4: VALUE (CONSUMER SPEND)/COSTS (TV)

But I can do better than point out when the good times were. I can use my schedule-writing program to investigate how total sales can be maximised over several years.

I use the values (food and drink combined) and the TV costs described, and other input, to calculate what the allocation over these years *should* be, for an advertiser who normally gets about 1,000 ratings a year. The results are given in Figure 5.

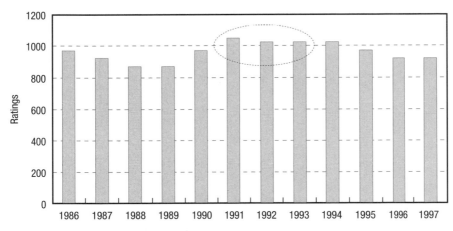

FIGURE 5: RECOMMENDED SCHEDULE

This suggests that 1991–94 should have had above-average ratings (1994 is probably included because there will be some carry-over into higher-cost 1995). The reasons why this would have been a sharp move are not connected with long-term effects – only with medium-term returns.

61

Figure 5 is very different from Figure 2. What no one seems to have appreciated is that, in the 1991-93 downturn, cost dropped a lot but values only a little.

Figure 5 also suggests that advertisers have been right to reduce rating levels as costs rise in the way they have done recently, but not to stop using TV. If hard times come, no dramatic increase in spend is looked for but certainly no cuts. The last point follows from a comparison of the sales expected from Figure 5 with those from an alternative strategy: not to spend in 1991–93, but reserve the total budget for 1986–90 and 1993–97. This cautious approach actually achieves 15% less advertising-produced sales over 1986–97. The timid are not smart marketers.

So my advice – as for scheduling within a year – is to pay attention to values/costs. You may find the benefit will be seen in increased ratings – and in sales, provided weaker competitors feel they cannot follow you.

From 'Tough Times', Simon Broadbent, *Admap*, April 1999.

PART TWO

Best Practice
Case Histories

Introduction to Part Two

Marilyn Baxter[1]

In Part Two we look at what we can learn about the theory from some best practice case histories. These are edited versions of full case histories from the IPA Data Bank of over 700 Advertising Effectiveness Awards cases produced since 1980. The six cases featured here have been selected as examples of companies and brands whose market and financial performance has benefited either from continuing Adspend or from increasing Adspend during an economic downturn. The six cases are:

Renault Clio
Whipsnade Wild Animal Park
De Beers
Barclaycard
Nescafé Gold Blend
BMW

Reasons for selection

The six cases have been selected on a number of criteria:

- They all cover a period that includes the last recession of the late 1980s/early 1990s
- They cover a wide variety of sectors
- They cover a wide variety of situations and roles for advertising
- They illustrate Professor Barwise's three positive strategies for dealing with recession: Look for New Opportunities (Clio, Whipsnade, De Beers); Strengthen Your Market Position Against Weaker Rivals (Barclaycard); and Keep Going (Gold Blend, BMW).

1. Marilyn Baxter is Vice Chairman of Saatchi & Saatchi and Chairman of the IPA's Value of Advertising Committee.

What do we expect to happen in a slowdown and what can advertising do about it?

In examining the relevance of these cases to learning how best to use advertising in a slowdown, we should first ask the question: What do we expect to happen in a slowdown?

In *durable products*, we would expect people to put off investment in new products, hold on to existing products for longer, and/or trade down to cheaper alternatives. In *fmcg* (fast moving consumer goods) *products*, we would expect people to trade down to cheaper/less good quality substitutes and to avoid the risk attached to buying new products. For *luxury/discretionary purchases* we would expect them to cut down on discretionary items and trade down to cheaper alternatives. And we might expect competitors to cut their marketing budgets, and so depress demand by removing the stimulus to buy.

So what can advertising do to counteract these effects? The cases illustrate specific examples, but in general terms advertising works by:

- Stimulating sales by providing a reason to buy
- Adding perceived value to trade off against relative high price
- Maintaining a price premium
- Informing persuasively about new products
- Taking advantage of competitors' budget cuts.

The value of these specific cases is to show for each brand the mechanism by which advertising produced results. Too often, companies cut Adspend as a knee-jerk reaction because they don't understand the mechanism by which it works, either on the short-term financial performance of the company or on long-term shareholder value. In each of these cases, the brand owner understood or believed as an act of faith the effect that advertising would have on short-term financial performance and/or on long-term brand equity. Unfortunately, because of the rules of the competition which generates these cases, authors are not required to give detailed financial performance data, but they do demonstrate share, sales and profitability improvements and calculate the payback of the Adspend.

It's not just what you do, it's also the way that you do it

Effective advertising results from a successful combination of creative strategy, creative ideas, media strategy and media expenditure. As these cases show, it is not always necessary to increase the ad budget in order to increase the effectiveness of the advertising. In fact, in most cases, the ad budget remained the same and was either deployed more effectively

TABLE 1: SUMMARY

Case	Sector	Role for advertising	Strategy for recession	Key results	Key learning
Renault Clio (1991)	Durables (cars)	Launch a new car with the second highest price point in the category, during the most severe recession in the sector	*Look for new opportunities.* Clear strategy of broadening the age profile of the appeal, executed through a very popular and powerful creative idea	• Exceeded first year's sales targets • Enhanced brand imagery and broadened age profile of owners • Established premium positioning • Improved sales mix to mid/top range models	• Advertising idea created an empathetic and desirable brand image in a market where it is hard to get real product differentiation • A great creative idea helps you ignore recession
Whipsnade Wild Animal Park (1990–92)	Leisure	Reverse long-term decline in visitor numbers caused by increased competition and historical lack of investment in promotion, in the depths of recession	*Look for new opportunities.* No change in product but ten-fold increase in budget (to £200k) spent on focused creative strategy and clever media planning	• 25% increase in visitors, despite price rise of 30% • Out-performed the competition, which suffered more from effects of recession	• Brave strategy paid off • Benefits of accurate targeting, in both media and creative
De Beers (1992–95)	Luxury goods (Diamonds)	Counter worldwide recessionary pressure by sustaining demand and thereby maintaining the stability of the industry	*Look for new opportunities.* Adopted a single ad campaign across 23 countries but no increase in ad budget	• Emotive campaign maintained and increased desirability of diamonds • Maintained stability of market and improved partnership with trade	• Possible to run successfully the same ad campaign around the world • Move to TV from press enhanced emotional message *and* saved production cost

(continued)

TABLE 1: SUMMARY (contd)

Case	Sector	Role for advertising	Strategy for recession	Key results	Key learning
Barclaycard (1989–91)	Financial services (credit cards)	Brand and market development against a background of net loss in 1990 in depth of recession – increase share – attract new users – justify the new fee	*Strengthen market position.* Introduced significant product improvements and doubled the ad budget at a time when competitor halved theirs	• Loss transformed to profit in midst of recession • 50% increase in share of new credit card holders • Turnover brand leader and growing	• Brave strategy paid off • Advertising added value to an improved product by translating features into benefits • Advertising added motivational value to DM campaign
Nescafé Gold Blend (1987–96)	Premium fmcg	Brand-building over the long term – broaden appeal to less upmarket users – justify price premium	*Keep going.* A ten-year advertising campaign with consistent spend throughout, allied to continuous product improvement and maintenance of price premium	• Increased sales of £50m p.a. from incremental ad budget of £5m p.a. • Doubled market share on unchanged adspend	• Powerful advertising idea drove brand preference and gave the brand a life beyond the product • Adspend does not pay back in short term (over one year), but growth has been compound and consistent. New buyers have become loyal buyers
BMW (GB) (1979–94)	Durables (cars)	Brand-building over the long term, extending appeal and creating strong consumer demand through richer brand imagery	*Keep going.* Consistency of product, brand values, high quality advertising and adspend over 15 years, regardless of recessions	• Adspend of £91m over 15 years helped create £3bn of extra sales • Strongest brand in UK car market and stronger in UK than in any other market	• Power of focused strategy and consistency of application • Contribution of brand imagery to consumer and trade loyalty and demand • Productivity of relatively low adspend

or spent behind a more powerful creative idea. Many of these featured cases demonstrate the extraordinary leverage that can be gained through advertising that captures the public's imagination and builds dimensions to the brand and its personality that no other part of the marketing mix can achieve.

Advertising alone is (generally) not enough

Most of the cases also illustrate the importance of advertising working with product or service improvements to achieve results; however, two (Whipsnade and De Beers) are 'pure' cases where there was no product improvement or change, and advertising alone achieved the results. Table 1 details the key features and key learning from the six cases.

The value of these cases is to illustrate the results that can be achieved from taking certain courses of action. Clearly, no case will parallel precisely any individual company's or brand's circumstances; it is not our intention to promote the argument 'If it worked for them, it will work for you', but rather to suggest that companies take these cases as references from which to examine their own businesses, and to learn more about the mechanisms by which advertising achieves its results.

About the IPA Case Histories Data Bank

The IPA Advertising Effectiveness Data Bank represents the most rigorous and comprehensive examination of advertising working in the marketplace, in the world. Over the 18 years of the IPA Advertising Effectiveness Awards Competition (1980–98), the IPA has collected over 700 examples of best practice in advertising development and results across a wide spectrum of marketing sectors and expenditures. Each example contains 4,000 words of text and is illustrated in full by market, research, sales and profit data.

Immediate access to the IPA Case Histories Data Bank can be gained through the World Advertising Research Center (WARC). Reached by logging on to www.WARC.com, the world's most comprehensive database enables readers to search the IPA case histories and thousands of other essential reference works by subject matter, author, date or virtually any other selection criteria. An online version of this report is also available. Further information on the World Advertising Research Center can be obtained from editor@warc.com or by telephoning +44 1491 418639.

CASE 1

Renault Clio: Adding Value during a Recession

Caroline Chandy and Douglas Thursby
(Publicis,1992)

In 1991 sales of new cars in the UK declined by 21%, the worst annual fall for 17 years. In March 1991 Renault UK launched the Clio, the successor to the long-established Renault 5. This paper sets out to demonstrate the effectiveness of the advertising campaign, first helping to launch the new car, then creating a premium positioning for it at the top of the small-car sector and finally broadening Renault's appeal in this sector, in terms of age profile.

Despite the unpropitious timing of its launch, the Clio succeeded in recapturing volume share for Renault in the small-car segment and delivering increased profit to the company through its premium price positioning.

Background

The small-car sector accounts for about 25% of UK new car sales and is the second most important sector in terms of volume. It is also, alongside the executive and luxury sector, the most influential in terms of shaping the manufacturer's overall marque image. The small-car sector is therefore of disproportionately high strategic significance and is growing in appeal.

Competition is strong with the three 'domestic' marques – Ford (Fiesta), Vauxhall (Nova) and Rover (Metro) – accounting for 57% of small-car sales in 1990; of these, both the Fiesta and Metro launched new models in 1990 immediately prior to the Clio launch. The other key competitor, the Peugeot 205, commanded a 10% share and was firmly established as the image leader in the sector.

The Renault 5 and the Clio Product

Launched in 1972, the extremely successful Renault 5 accounted in its prime for 41% of Renault sales in the UK. However, by 1990 it was showing its age in the face of more dynamic competition, its sector share declining to 4.1% and its sector ranking falling to ninth position.

The Clio was a *replacement* for the Renault 5 – a totally new car, not a facelift. For the launch, three core variants would be available: the entry model 1.1 litre RL, the 1.2 litre RN and the 1.4 litre RT.

The Clio's main point of competitive difference was that it brought a new standard of refinement to the small-car sector. However, as has often been proved, strong product advantage does not in itself guarantee sales success (cf. Fiat Tipo); a developed brand image is essential.

Issues

Entry Prices

The Clio's entry price was £1,200 higher than for the Renault 5. In the small-car sector, only the Honda Civic had a higher entry price. Prior to the Clio, Renault's price positioning was at the middle to lower end of the sector where it was perceived to offer good value for money. Indeed, price was the primary reason given for purchasing a Renault 5 in 1990. The Clio advertising would need to play its part in justifying Renault's new premium pricing in the sector – without alienating Renault 5 owners.

The Recession

At the time of the Clio launch, consumer confidence for major purchases remained depressed – sales of new cars in the UK had been falling for 18 consecutive months. The first months of 1991 also saw a 'price war' in both the small and lower-medium car sectors, with prices in the lower-medium becoming competitive against small cars. These were not ideal conditions in which to launch a premium-priced small car.

Health of the Renault Marque

The role of the marque image plays an important part within the individual model purchasing decision. A marque that is neither desired nor respected can prevent a model from being placed on a shopping list. Qualitative research in 1990 revealed that, although Renault had attained 'first division' status in terms of product acceptability, the key problem was a lack of *positive* image factors resulting in low desirability. It was clear that, at launch, the Clio would not benefit from strong parent brand endorsement. The parent and the new model would have to develop in tandem.

The business objectives
Sales and Marketing Objectives
Renault UK set the Clio the following sales objectives:

1. To achieve 1.38% of the total car market (5.5% of the sector).
2. To account for 33% of Renault sales.

Both these objectives were to be achieved by the end of the first full year of trading. In effect, the Clio was required to emulate the Renault 5's 1989 sales performance from year one.

The marketing objectives set for the Clio were:

1. To retain the loyalty of a high percentage of Renault 5 owners.
2. To steal share from key competitive models.

The marketing strategy set out to launch a highly specified Clio at a high entry price, supported by heavyweight theme advertising and substantial below-the-line activity.

The advertising strategy
Advertising Objectives

1. To announce the new Renault Clio.
2. To establish a premium positioning for the Clio in the small-car sector.
3. To broaden Renault's appeal in the small-car sector in terms of age profile.

Targeting and positioning
Core buyers in the small-car sector are typically ABC1 professionals aged 25–44 years with a fairly even male/female split. In terms of age, Renault 5 had a purchaser profile four years younger than the sector average. However, given the Clio's premium status, it was decided to broaden its age appeal. The target audience was expanded to all those aged 25 years plus and thereby also included those aged 45 years and over.

The potential Clio buyer was identified as being slightly out of the car-buying mainstream, coming out of a broader age spectrum and displaying greater attitudinal *joie de vivre* than his or her standard counterpart. This proved highly directive in developing a differentiating brand personality for the Clio.

Further research conducted across Europe revealed that, on the Continent too – though for differing reasons – small-car buyers were increasingly demanding the 'extras' normally associated with executive cars. As a result, Renault adopted the following pan-European brand positioning:

> *The small car with the refinement of a big car.*

The campaign
The advertising campaign was planned in two phases:

Announcement phase: To run for only two weeks, the announcement phase was restricted to two objectives:

- To create maximum awareness of the arrival of the new Clio from Renault.
- To make a stylistic break from previous Renault advertising in this sector and so begin the process of consumer reappraisal.

The creative executions were built around the concept of a car hatching from a technological egg (quite apposite as the UK launch was on Easter weekend), symbolising the birth of a new car, with the line 'Not just another hatch'.

Positioning phase: The role of this phase was three-fold: to position the car, to build a long-term and lasting image for the Clio, and to continue to enhance consumer awareness.

To this end a 60-second commercial, made specifically for the UK by Publicis London, was aired. The storyline follows the supposedly clandestine extracurricular activities of a father (Papa) visiting his mistress, and his daughter (Nicole) visiting her boyfriend. The Clio RT was featured in both instances in the role of an accomplice. In the commercial, Nicole serves to epitomise the generic small-car values of fun, youth and nippiness, whilst Papa serves to broaden the age appeal of the car and reflect the added refinement of the new Clio. The commercial ended with the new marque strapline, '*Renault: A Certain Flair*'.

The commercial was aired for two more bursts in summer and autumn, cut down to 40 seconds and 30 seconds respectively. During periods without television activity, two full-page colour advertisements were rotated in the national press while double-page versions appeared in the colour supplements and specialist car magazines. In all, 66% of the media spend in the first nine months was put into TV, 29% into press, and 4% into posters.

The sales results

Despite the depressed state of the car market in 1991, the Clio exceeded its first year sales objectives. Its success boosted Renault's small-car sector share to 7.7%, and its total marque share to 4.0%, in both cases Renault's best figures since 1981. In attaining a total market share of 1.82%, the Clio surpassed the equivalent performance of both its predecessor, the Renault Super 5, and its most immediate competitor, the Peugeot 205, which recorded first-year market shares of 1.65% and 1.09% respectively.

The first year of Clio sales also saw the middle and top-of-the-range versions (RN/RT) accounting for a higher proportion of the sales mix than had been the case for the Renault 5 (76% of sales compared to 57% for the Renault 5). This shift in the mix provided an early endorsement of the changed positioning as well as increased profit to the company.

Evaluating the campaign

The protracted nature of the buying process, the role of the dealer, the amount of other marketing activity that accompanies a new car launch (motor shows, direct mailing, PR coverage), the role of product quality, and the difficulty of organising any kind of regional test, all make isolating the precise effects of the Clio launch campaign fiendishly difficult. This paper therefore concentrates on the traditional advertising and brand response measures in order to establish whether the advertising objectives were met, and so attempts to draw a connection between the advertising and subsequent sales performance, but does not attempt to separate out the effects of advertising from other parts of the marketing mix.

Advertising measures

Advertising Awareness

There was a considerable build of claimed awareness of the Clio advertising, reaching a peak of 56% in May 1991, which then stabilised to around 40% for the rest of the year. Both the launch and 'Papa and Nicole' commercials were highly effective in generating brand associated recall. Both commercials attained a Millward Brown Awareness Index of 7, well above the average of 3–4 for all car advertising.

Brand Identification

Both commercials succeeded in achieving higher levels of correct model and marque identification than the best performing advertising for the Renault 5: 65% correctly recalled the 'Papa and Nicole' commercial as being Renault and 50% correctly recalled the model name 'Clio'.

We believe that one of the key reasons for the success of this campaign was the use, in the 'Papa and Nicole' commercial, of 'Structural Branding'. Having identified that the potential Clio buyer was attitudinally different from most of the car-buying public, it was critically important, in terms of casting, that the central characters in the commercial reflect this attitudinal difference. Strong branding was created and achieved for the Clio by successfully 'marrying' the personalities of the main characters with the inherent personality of the marque.

Attitudes to the Advertising

In terms of prompted attitudes, both commercials were favoured by consumers, especially 'Papa and Nicole'. Of the sample, 80% positively endorsed the commercial compared with an average of 58% for all car commercials in 1991.

In this context, it is interesting to examine the recent Copy Research Validity Project carried out by the American Advertising Research Foundation, in which they concluded that *'the most surprising finding in the study was the strong relationship found to exist between the likeability of the copy and its effect on sales'.*

We also know that the behaviour and attitude of dealer staff is often linked to what they perceive to be (or not to be) 'effective' and 'consumer-liked' advertising. (For this reason a close relationship with a 'Dealer Panel' was maintained in the development of the campaign.)

Qualitative research since the launch has confirmed how well liked the Clio advertising has become; a point further endorsed by the large PR and press coverage the campaign has attracted.

Brand measures

Brand Awareness

Two months after launch, spontaneous brand awareness of the Clio compared well with other car launches, including that of the Renault 19 two years earlier (Table 1).

TABLE 1

	Spontaneous awareness (2 months after launch) (1)	Share of voice (2)	Ratio (1 + 2)
Clio	5	6.30	0.79
Renault 19	5	7.25	0.68
Average of 8 launches	2	6.10	0.33

Source: Millward Brown, MEAL

Obviously, advertising is not the only contributor to brand awareness; other communication channels such as dealer promotions, PR, direct marketing, etc., all play a significant role. An analysis of model awareness by advertising recall however shows a marked increase in awareness of the Clio by those claiming to have seen the advertising against those who have not.

Renault's Customerlink Survey reported that television advertising received the highest number of mentions for prompting buyers' initial interest in the Clio and was the second most influential source of additional information (once initial interest had been aroused). These scores for the Clio were well ahead of those achieved by other Renault models.

Brand Image

Brand image was also monitored by the Millward Brown Tracking Study. One might have expected the Clio, as a new car, to take some time to establish an image profile, but in fact this was quickly achieved. An analysis of the perceived strengths and weaknesses of the Clio relative to other cars in the small-car sector reveals a strong and differentiated image centred around style but also driveability and roominess; in other words, *'big car refinement'*.

New Car Buyers Survey (NCBS) asked Renault buyers why they bought what they did. The reasons given for purchasing a Clio show key strengths to be: 'style', 'spaciousness' and 'equipment'. This contrasted strongly with the reasons given for purchasing a Renault 5, and highlighted how a distinct different overall positioning for the Clio had been created, so justifying its high entry price point.

Source of Business
Purchaser data for the first five weeks of sales showed that 52% of Clio sales were bought in replacement of another Renault and 44% were conquest sales. First-time or additional buyers accounted for the remaining 5% of sales. These early results indicated that a reassuring level of loyalty to the marque was being achieved despite the Clio's different positioning from the Renault 5.

Driver Profile
A key objective was for the advertising to extend the Clio's appeal to a broader, older age group than the Renault 5. This was clearly achieved with Clio drivers on average being seven years older than the segment and 14 years older than Renault 5 buyers.

Conclusion
The Clio not only met but also exceeded its first year sales targets. This was achieved in a marketplace which, in 1991, saw sales down by one-fifth on 1990 with even the small-car sector down by 18%. In its first full year of trading, the Clio helped Renault to achieve both its highest small-car sector share and its highest overall marque share in a decade.

The advertising campaign contributed to the development of a new premium positioning for Renault in the small-car sector, in mid-recession and without alienating Renault owners, thus helping to meet a major and difficult marketing objective while generating increased profit for the company. Furthermore, it helped widen the age profile of buyers, in a sector where Renault had historically attracted younger owners. It was also shown to be the key source of initial interest for eventual buyers.

We believe that this stemmed from the correct identification of the attitudinal motivations of an 'individual' target audience and its consequent application in the course of the positioning phase of the campaign through the adoption of 'Structural Branding'. This created an empathetic and desirable brand image for the Clio in a market where inter-product differentiation is becoming increasingly difficult. Results from all aspects of evaluation suggest that the effectiveness of the advertising campaign has played a major role in the successful launch of the car.

Whipsnade Wild Animal Park: How TV Advertising Helped Reverse a 30-year Decline

Cathy Clift
(Lowe Howard-Spink, 1992)

Whipsnade Wild Animal Park has been in long-term decline since its peak in the 1960s. This paper shows how a bold strategy of using television advertising has reversed this 30-year trend and sustained the recovery despite adverse economic conditions which have seen all of Whipsnade's major competitors in decline.

Whipsnade's declining fortunes

Whipsnade Wild Animal Park is the 'country home' of the Zoological Society of London and harbours over 2,800 animals, including many rare and endangered species.

Whipsnade has seen annual attendances decline from 750,000 in 1961 to 380,000 in 1989. Whipsnade's management attributed this decline to the failure, over many years, to attract new generations of visitors to Whipsnade. In turn, this was attributed to two main factors:

- The growth in local, heavily advertised, competitors such as Windsor Safari Park and Chessington World of Adventures. These combined wild animals with the added attractions of rides and amusements.
- A chronic lack of investment by Whipsnade in advertising and promotion.

The advertising challenge

Lowe Howard-Spink was appointed in January 1990. The advertising brief was simple: to help increase visitor numbers.

The year 1989 had been Whipsnade's worst-ever season for attendances. Despite the favourable circumstances of a long, hot summer, visitor numbers had fallen 11% on the previous year to 380,000. Whipsnade's marketing objective was to reverse the long-term decline and raise attendances by 26%, an increase of 33% over the number of visitors predicted by the 30-year trend.

The advertising strategy

Both Whipsnade's own visitor records and market data collected by the British Tourist Authority (BTA) indicated that Whipsnade competes in the 'Family Day Out' category of visitor attractions. The market for family days out embraces a diverse range of destinations and experiences, from theme parks such as Alton Towers, through to a trip to the zoo, or a day at the seaside. Qualitative research revealed that such days out fall broadly into two subcategories: those initiated by children and often described by parents as 'junk' entertainment; and those initiated by parents and seen by them as having more 'nutritious', that is, educational, value.

We had no ambitions to try to relocate Whipsnade in the 'junk' sector competing on the same terms as theme parks. This would not only have grossly misrepresented the nature of the Whipsnade experience but would also have conflicted with its scientific role as a centre for conservation and rare species breeding. The strategy, therefore, was to boost its performance in the 'educational days out' sector. The key decision-makers in this sector are parents, not children, so parents were to be the primary target of the advertising campaign. However, we also needed to take care not to alienate children, since they still have veto power in such situations.

In the light of this decision, we then had to ask where Whipsnade stood in the marketplace. Prompted recognition of the Whipsnade name was high (89% in London and 79% in Central TV region). Although the levels of spontaneous mentions were naturally much lower (34% in London and 15% in Central), they were broadly comparable with Windsor and Chessington, each of which received approximately three times more visitors than Whipsnade. Clearly, the problem was not simply one of awareness.

Qualitative research, comparing the views of Whipsnade visitors with demographically similar groups of non-visitors, revealed that although the name 'Whipsnade' itself was familiar enough, potential visitors had only the haziest idea of what kind of day out Whipsnade would offer. Many still thought of it as a zoo (which had indeed been its official title until recently). This conjured up images of Victorian menageries and animals in cages. Equally, the term 'Wild Animal Park' was for many people indistinguishable from 'Safari Park' – of which Windsor was by far the best-known example and already widely visited.

The role for advertising was not simply to make Whipsnade more 'top of mind' among parents planning a family day out, but also to create a strong and distinctive character for the place, which would earn it a unique position on their list of 'places to go'.

The creative solution

The key features which give Whipsnade its unique character are the animals themselves and their environment. It has over 100 species of wild and rare animals, in a naturally beautiful setting, where they live in their natural social groups, behaving as though in the wild. We believed that this strongly differentiated Whipsnade from purely commercial theme parks, where the main attractions are rides and amusements, and the animals are essentially a side-show.

In the creative brief, the appeal that we wished to communicate was summarised as:

A walk on the wild side.

A 40-second TV commercial was created in 1990 to capture the beauty and excitement of the Whipsnade experience. Based on the film *Out of Africa*, it comprised a series of shots of wild and exotic animals behaving completely naturally, apparently in their native habitat, and only at the end is it revealed that the entire film was shot on location at Whipsnade Wild Animal Park, *'Out of Bedfordshire'*.

The media strategy

Because Whipsnade is an outdoor attraction, the vast majority of new visitors would need to be attracted between April and September. Moreover, there are for Whipsnade (in common with most other domestic visitor attractions in the UK), 20 key days a year which can account for up to 30% of the year's total visitor revenue. These are the bank holiday weekends, beginning with Easter and ending with the last weekend in August.

Although Whipsnade was operating on a small budget, we believed that only television could provide the impact and fast coverage needed to achieve our objectives. The TV plan for Whipsnade was based on three factors which had been clarified in research:

- typically the decision to visit an attraction is made only a short time before the visit, but a candidate list is drawn up beforehand from which the final choice is made depending on mood or the weather;
- certain weekends, including bank holidays, were key, so the plan was built around these;
- most visitors live within one hour's drive time of Whipsnade, in the London, Central and Anglia TV regions. Initially, Central was judged to be the best region to concentrate on (given our limited funds) for cost and frequency reasons, and the 1990 campaign was confined to Central. But it emerged from research that in fact London (despite its higher cost) and Anglia (despite its sparse population) would be likely to generate higher proportions of visitors. The second half of the TV campaign was therefore redeployed from Central into London and Anglia.

A 10-second commercial was created to run with the original 40-second film in the ratio of 1:1. This enabled us to buy more spots in the London region and also to extend our TV presence back earlier into the week preceding a bank holiday.

Although less than half of competitive spend levels, the £200,000 budget represented a ten-fold increase on Whipsnade's historical advertising spend. This had previously concentrated on attracting visitors from the immediate locality by promoting special events such as birds of prey displays, Easter egg hunts, etc. on Chiltern Radio. However, whereas the TV advertising was intended to attract new visitors, it was felt that the promotion of special events on Chiltern Radio still had a complementary role to play in giving local and regular visitors a reason to revisit. Accordingly, Whipsnade's spend on local radio was fully maintained.

What have we achieved?

In 1990, the number of visitors to Whipsnade increased by 25%, from 380,000 in 1989 to 473,000. This marked a dramatic reversal of the long-term decline in attendance (see Figure 1).

Regular surveys of visitors indicated that a major element of this growth had come from an increased proportion of 'new' visitors (ie those who had never before visited or had not visited for over ten years), which had risen from 48% at the beginning of the season to 60% by the end.

Whipsnade Wild Animal Park

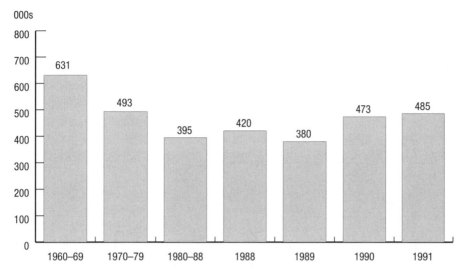

FIGURE 1: ANNUAL VISITOR NUMBERS
Source: Whipsnade Wild Animal Park

In 1991 visitor numbers rose to 485,000, despite the adverse economic conditions (recession and increased mortgage rates), which saw a real reduction in leisure spending in 1991 of nearly 2% over 1990. This sustained improvement by Whipsnade over the two years is in marked contrast to the fortunes of Whipsnade's strongest local competitors from whom it was clearly stealing share (Table 1).

TABLE 1: WHIPSNADE OUTPERFORMS THE COMPETITION
(visitor numbers indexed against 1989)

	Whipsnade	Chessington	Windsor	Thorpe Park
1989	100	100	100	100
1990	125	122	97	76
1991	128	115	82	72

Source: BTA, WWAP

Only Chessington came close to Whipsnade's 1989–90 increase in visitors and no competitor managed to hold firm from 1990 to 1991.

Furthermore, this achievement was sustained despite a 32% increase in the gate price, from Easter 1991, which took the price of an adult admission from £4.50 to £5.95.

How do we know it was TV advertising that made the difference?

Evidence for the central role of TV advertising in increasing Whipsnade's attendances is derived primarily from visitor surveys throughout the 1990 and 1991 summer seasons. Each wave sampled 300 visitors around key weekends such as bank holidays and at the beginning of school summer holidays in July.

This research provides three indicators of a correlation between advertising activity and visitor numbers:

1. Profile of visitors by ITV region.
2. TV advertising awareness by ITV region.
3. Claimed 'influence of advertising on decision to visit' by ITV region.

Most importantly, the data show not just that each of these indicators moved in line with the others, but also that the change in media strategy during 1990 was accurately reflected in changes across all three indicators.

1. Profile of Whipsnade Visitors by ITV Region

The percentage of visitors from Central TV region reached its peak of 20% at the end of May 1990. This coincides with the last of the three bursts of activity on Central. Since then there has been no further advertising on Central. The proportion of visitors from that region fell rapidly, to settle at approximately half the peak. Correspondingly, the percentage of visitors who claim to watch London or Anglia TV stations most often has growth significantly since the change in media strategy, from the low 1970s to the mid-1980s.

2. Awareness of TV Advertising

Awareness of TV advertising has mirrored the visitor profile results. When we were on-air in Central, claimed awareness of TV advertising built to 41%. Since coming off-air in Central, awareness has declined to around 14%. In London it rose quickly from 8% to 35% and has remained at around that level. Awareness in Anglia has grown steadily from 4% to 34%.

3. Influence of Advertising on Decision to Visit

Although in some respects this is a naive question which can seriously underestimate the true influence of advertising on purchase behaviour, we decided to ask it nonetheless. The earliest results, at the beginning of the first season, suggest that the advertising was influential while on air, but that this influence was rapidly eroded between bursts. The 1991 results suggest that the commercial has gained in effectiveness with repeated exposure over two seasons ('wear-in') and our expectation would be that this would produce more carry-over effect between bursts than it did initially.

Again, a comparison between results for visitors from the different ITV regions, receiving different weights of advertising over time, indicates that this influence is associated with TV advertising rather than any other promotional activity. In particular, the Anglia airtime appears to have been very cost-effective – all the more remarkable considering that in choosing the Anglia West transmitter, we were restricted to only seven spots a week. These spots were always immediately after the regional news, however, and it can be argued that this particular programme environment found audiences in an especially receptive mood.

What else could have contributed to the rise in visitor numbers?

There are three other potential factors: relative price, weather, and 'product'. Each of these plays a part in the decision of where to go for a day out. Nonetheless, they can all be eliminated as important agents of the growth in visitors to Whipsnade.

Relative Price

Whipsnade has not reduced its prices in order to attract more visitors. On the contrary, in 1991 it raised its ticket prices by 32%. No competitor has raised its admission prices by more than 12% since 1989.

Weather

The summer of 1990 was one of the sunniest on record, and this is certain to have had a positive effect on visitor numbers. However, 1989 had been at least as good a summer as 1990, yet it marked the nadir of Whipsnade's fortunes. Equally, the summer of 1991 was one of the dullest on record, yet attendances actually rose slightly.

'Product' Quality

Can the increase in visitor numbers be attributed to any significant improvements in the quality of the 'product'? Regular surveys of 'visitor satisfaction' over the 1990 and 1991 seasons show that visitor satisfaction levels have remained virtually unchanged over the period.

The payback

The primary aim of advertising Whipsnade on television was to dramatically increase visitor numbers and revenue.

A media investment of £500,000 over two years has generated the major part of a 26% increase in attendances over the same period, and the incremental revenue from these extra visitors and the higher entry price they were willing to pay has taken Whipsnade from a financial loss of £1.3 million in 1989 to an anticipated profit of £0.4 million in 1992.

Although this forms no part of our case for the effectiveness of Whipsnade's advertising, the Chief Executive, Mr Andrew Forbes, also believes that the increased visibility and popularity of Whipsnade *'has awakened the corporate sector who now see us as a positive proposition'*. This has helped Whipsnade negotiate some important sponsorship deals with major UK companies to support new visitor attractions and also to build a Conservation and Breeding Centre.

De Beers – 'Hard Times: Selling Diamonds in a Recession': How a Great British Idea Worked Across Europe and Beyond

Merry Baskin
(J Walter Thompson, 1996)

This paper demonstrates how a change in advertising strategy, execution and deployment, unifying 23 countries under a single approach, during one of the worst economic recessions, worked to build shareholder and trade confidence and maintain a healthy balance between short-term sales and long-term image exclusivity among consumers.

There are several reasons why this case is uniquely interesting: there is no brand *per se* and every product is a one-off over whose finished form, design, price, packaging and distribution system the client has no control; there is a dual target audience with differing needs and motivations in 23 disparate countries; this is not a case of a demonstrable link between advertising effectiveness and client profitability, but rather one where advertising has worked to maintain *viability* for its sponsor and *stability* for an entire industry worldwide.

Background to the diamond business

Mining is a long-term project, and diamond producers are not in the business of short-term profits. On average, 250 tons of ore have to be dug out in order to produce one carat of polished gem diamond.

Gem diamonds have no functional value whatsoever, and because they are not an essential commodity like oil, demand and prices can be erratic. It was for this reason that De Beers founded the Central Selling Organisation (CSO) in the 1930s, which has agreements with the major diamond-producing nations to purchase and value all their production of rough diamonds at controlled prices (amounting to 80% of world production).

Selling their production through De Beers gives the diamond-producing nations greater financial stability to underpin the cost of mining. But unless there is consumer demand for diamond jewellery, the rising cost of its stockpile could arguably bankrupt De Beers. Feeding rough diamonds into the pipeline is the start; the commercial necessity is to keep the polished product moving out. In order to generate this consumer 'pull-through', De Beers undertakes the advertising and promotion of diamond jewellery around the globe on behalf of the diamond industry, in co-operation with the jewellery trade, whose representatives cut, polish, design, set and retail the finished product.

Diamond jewellery is clearly a non-essential luxury product. It has a broad competitive set: holidays, fridge freezers, mortgages, investments, the children, throwing a party, watches, and other precious coloured stone jewellery. In the US, cubic zirconium, which looks the same to the untrained eye at a fraction of the price, is added to the list. In the East, there is major competition from gold, which serves many purposes beyond social display, both as an investment and a form of currency.

Global slump

The diamond business has traditionally been inextricably tied to the economy. There is a close relationship between GDP and consumer confidence, and between consumer confidence and sales of diamond jewellery. Our econometric model shows an excellent fit of 0.97894 (a perfect fit being 1.0).

A severe recession hit GDP in major markets from 1988–89. People switched from spending to saving. Jewellers continued to sell what they could, but de-stocked. Had this trend continued, it would have led to reduced sales in the long term due to a combination of a reduced saliency of diamond jewellery with a more limited choice of jewellery. De Beers therefore had to take steps to prevent the potential dramatic erosion of diamond jewellery sales.

Business and advertising objectives

The role for advertising by the Central Selling Organisation is to manage effectively the esteem (and value) with which diamonds are perceived around the world. Historically, this has been achieved via the 'gift of love' positioning, and the development of diamond traditions or occasions, such as the 'Sweet Ten' anniversary ring in Japan.

The challenge is for diamonds to 'own' these occasions, to the extent that consumers believe the cash investment to be *emotionally*, rather than financially, rewarding. Advertising is used to present the core values of diamonds (beauty, rarity, uniqueness, brilliance, purity, everlasting durability) via their emotional specialness (gift of love).

The 1992–93 business objective for De Beers was to protect sales related to core 'occasions' business segments in the face of deepening worldwide recession. This could be achieved by one of two routes according to market development.

1. By maximising the return from the *mature* markets via consumers 'trading up' to more expensive pieces. This definition includes the UK, US and Italy, where diamond ownership is around 70%. (It is important to note that the higher the retail price, the higher the percentage of diamond content within the retail price paid. You cannot add much more gold to a ring; you can add a lot more diamond.)
2. By growing *developing* markets via increased penetration of diamond jewellery ownership. This 'acquisition' definition includes markets like Thailand, Mexico and the Gulf where gold is strong but diamond traditions are less well established. In Thailand, for instance, penetration is 5.5%, and concentrated in cities.

The advertising objectives were set as:

1. To strengthen diamond jewellery's position as the ultimate gift of love in the face of a continued recession and increased competition.
2. To translate those positive attitudes into purchase behaviour.

Limited Funds

De Beers spends around 0.4% of the value of world diamond jewellery sales on marketing. This is a considerably smaller percentage than other luxury goods advertisers, but unfortunately there was no significant budget increase to help address the task. We believed that a cost-effective way of doing this might be to adopt Marshall McLuhan's 'one world, one ad' policy. But could we pull it off, given the variety of cultures and religions within 23 markets?

Countries where 'Shadows' has run					
Australia	Germany	Oman	Thailand	Austria	Holland
Philippines	Turkey	Belgium	Italy	Russia	UAE
Brazil	Japan	Saudi Arabia	UK	Canada	Kuwait
Spain	USA	France	Mexico	South Africa	

Historical, Cultural and Religious Differences

A few examples illustrate this diversity.

Engagement. Within Europe, 70% of UK couples currently buy diamond engagement rings, whereas in Germany, there is no engagement ring tradition.

Marriage. In Islamic circles, bridal sets (comprising necklace, earrings, bracelet and ring) symbolise parental care and are given by both sets of parents as a nest-egg for the bride.

Other occasions. US traditions include the 'Sweet 16' diamond for fathers to give their daughters in recognition of their transition to womanhood, and a diamond on the birth of a child.

Other jewels. Japan has historically had a pearl-based jewel tradition. There was no Japanese word for diamond until the 1960s.

Other precious metals. In Eastern cultures, from Turkey to the Far East, everything revolves around gold as a form of security or portable wealth.

Summary of Advertising Challenges

- To unify all the important mature and developing countries under a single approach, flexible enough to recognise local needs.
- To identify a single powerful consumer motivation across Europe, Asia, the Gulf, USA, Australia and South America.
- To provide executional guidance to enhance the creative idea for each market.

The creative brief

The line 'A diamond is forever' was first penned in the US in 1947, but was being taken for granted, and without revitalisation would not stop recession-conscious customers from putting off the purchase or trading down to a coloured (eg sapphire or ruby) stone piece. In the East, where diamond jewellery is less well established as a love symbol, the line is imbued with less romantic meaning.

Whatever the individual market idiosyncrasies, the role of diamond jewellery is the same – the giver expressing the enduring love they felt for the recipient and the joy the recipient would feel receiving and wearing such a gift. However, we still had to find a means of expressing this in a much more powerful way. The creative teams were asked to focus on the moment of giving rather than wearing, as this seemed to be the most emotionally charged (and rewarding) moment for our dual audience of giver and receiver.

A Change in Media
Historically, De Beers ran predominantly women's print campaigns. Now, the recession demanded more aggressive consumer media to ratchet up the emotional response to the 'ultimate gift of love' message. We chose TV and cinema to:

- reach a broader target audience, watching 'together' as
  couples, and evoke a strong emotional response between them
  simultaneously;
- exploit the added power of moving images and sound.

The main target audience was adults aged 25+, although engagement ring cinema audiences were slightly younger. Due to the length of the purchase cycle, we deployed a drip-buying policy of quality programming to achieve high saliency levels.

Production Values
Each market used to produce its own print campaigns of between two and ten different executions. Photographing diamonds, especially against skin, is notoriously difficult; print production quality was always an expensive challenge. Historically, the estimated annual worldwide print production budget for De Beers had been in excess of US$1.5 million.

For television, the use of new techniques with lasers and fibre-optic lighting combined with the stark contrast of shadows provided the ideal backdrop to display the scintillation of each individual stone. The production costs for the first three TV executions which ran for over three years were US$700,000. Thus the advertising was both more effective in communicating the appeal of diamond jewellery and more cost-effective to produce.

The Creative Idea

The power of the resultant 'Shadows' idea lies in the anonymity of the people and the setting, and the prominent showcasing of the jewellery at the musically climactic moment of giving. This apparently simple device carries a complex raft of messages and associations. Consumer feedback about the worth, desirability and suitability of diamond jewellery emanated from these elements:

- *The powerful music track* captured the attention and communicated drama, emotion and romance.
- *The visual intrigue of the shadows* was involving; something to decipher and imagine.
- *The anonymity of the shadows* was also mysterious, romantic and potentially 'me'! Race, colour, class and age are all irrelevant when you are a shadow. This was key to the cross-cultural acceptance of the communication.
- *The sophistication of black and white* stood out amidst colour commercials.
- *The story* encapsulated a relationship. Consumers wanted it to happen to them; it was simultaneously involving and aspirational.

The production technique was a *dramatic showcase* for the product: big, beautiful and highly desirable.

Evaluation of the campaign

Positive Consumer Response

Spontaneous advertising recall and prompted recognition of the 'Shadows' campaign has continued to build in all markets surveyed while the campaign has been on-air. The campaign has a universally high 'likeability' rating across all markets, a measurement that De Beers feels is important in creating advertising to enhance the desirability of diamond jewellery.

Attitude statements about diamond jewellery, tracked over time by market, have remained constant or improved since 'Shadows' started. The 'gift of love' significance has been particularly strengthened in Japan and the US, and diamonds' suitability to mark important occasions has grown in the UK, Italy and the US. Diamonds' position versus gold in the Gulf has also improved significantly.

The desirability of diamond jewellery has been maintained over time and it has suffered very little in Europe as a result of belt-tightening or postponement, and not at all in the overseas markets.

Diamond Acquisition Rates/Trading Up

Since 'Shadows', acquisition decline has been arrested and average price has increased, thus confirming the success of the trade-up strategy. An exception is Italy, where the average price has increased since the advertising began.

Analysis of the relationship between retail value and average price further confirms the success of the trade-up strategy. When retail value appears to have declined but the average price has increased (or decreased to a lesser degree), this indicates that the consumer has increased the diamond content of their jewellery. This has occurred in the UK, Italy, Germany and Spain.

Comparative Competitive Performance – Gold Jewellery

Between 1993 and 1995, the value of plain gold jewellery sales in Europe fell by 2% while total gold jewellery rose by 8%. In terms of pieces sold, both segments saw increases of 23% and 17% respectively. This implies that European consumers were buying more, but less expensive, plain gold pieces, while increasing their purchase of more expensive gem-set jewellery items. Our trade panel data tell us that four-fifths of value sales contain diamonds, and two-fifths of the pieces.

In Saudi Arabia, which accounts for 60% of Gulf gold consumption, the value growth of gold jewellery has been in gem-set gold. Similar dramatic increases are shown for the number of pieces bought containing gems since the campaign started. In the United States, total gold jewellery value (containing gems) has increased, while the number of pieces has declined again, indicating trade up.

Trade Enthusiasm and Support

De Beers runs a trade association in key markets, called the Carat Club. Members are from the leaders in the local diamond industry: retailers, designers and wholesalers. The latest membership survey conducted at the end of 1995/early 1996 illustrates their enthusiasm for the 'Shadows' campaign, an acknowledgement from a normally grudging audience of its positive effect on their business. Here a few comments illustrate the point:

UK

> *'The market was in the doldrums, and people were buying on price. Ratners had created this market of "flash for cash" and the "Shadows" campaign has lifted the cartage sales quite considerably.'*

(Kjeld Jacobsen, MD of Argenta Design, Jeweller/Manufacturer)

Germany

> *'The De Beers campaign reaches the soul of the consumer. This is the only way of selling more high-quality diamond jewellery in Germany.'*

(Dr Andreas Freisfeld, Owner, Cadoro Jeweller Group)

USA

> *'I feel the "Shadows" campaign has increased diamond jewellery sales quite dramatically. For example, not only did our diamond engagement rings increase by 15% but the sell-through at the retail level increased a dramatic 25%. This campaign has also helped in the sale of larger centre stones which, in turn, has created higher price point sales.'*

(Arthur D'Annunzio, D'Annunzio and Co, diamond jewellery manufacturer)

Gulf

> *'The advertising has raised consumers' curiosity about diamonds. They are now more interested to come into the shop to enquire about diamonds. In the past it used to be all about gold, now more ask about diamond jewellery.'*

(Baksh, Saudi Arabia)

Quantitative evidence from the US shows how in 1996 De Beers' advertising took the number one slot ahead of the economy for the first time, in trade acknowledgement of its role as a positive influence over diamond jewellery sales.

Sales Maintained in Spite of Confidence Levels

As explained earlier, one of the key measures affecting sales of diamond jewellery in a recession is consumer confidence. Prior to and during the campaign, consumer confidence was affected by international economic issues as well as domestic ones. Diamond retail value responded to the 'Shadows' advertising run during the recession in the respective countries by bucking the consumer confidence trend levels and maintaining a steady growth. The econometric model shows that the advertising improved sales by 2% above expected levels in the first year, rising to 14% by the end of 1995. This gives a three-year campaign average of +8% in sales, accounting for $2,715 million additional retail sales in the US for that period compared with a US advertising budget for the period of $113 million.

The US is a large and mature market and the same sales response to the advertising has not applied across the rest of the world. Nevertheless, the worldwide marketing spend of $558 million (80% on 'Shadows' advertising) is felt to have been well invested by De Beers' management:

> *Despite the sluggish performance of the global economy in 1993 the combined profits of De Beers (Group) recovered by 21% to US$595 million. This satisfactory outcome owed something to the beginnings of renewed growth in retail sales. It owed far more, however, to the successful (marketing) measures taken by the CSO to restore stability and confidence to the market. The crisis that had threatened in 1992 was averted.*

(Chairman's Statement, Annual Report 1993)

> *'Whatever short-term shocks we have absorbed, the long-term trend has been one of ever-increasing demand for polished diamonds. The diamond market did not "just grow". We have been involved in its development through careful and targeted stimulation by our consumer marketing division. This year we will spend about 4% of our turnover on nurturing demand for the product you sell – the polished diamond – and we think this is money well spent.'*

(Nicholas Oppenheimer, World Diamond Congress, Tel Aviv, 28 May 1996)

What else could have explained the sales success?

'People do not stop getting married and having children just because there is a recession on. De Beers would have sold just as many diamonds anyway.'

The close links between these 'rites of passage' have been successfully created by De Beers' advertising in the first place. But outside of the mature Western markets of Europe and the US, these 'rites of passage' occasions are *not* well established, and in all markets, gold, coloured stones and cubic zirconium can represent a very viable consumer jewellery alternative.

'It's a monopoly and they control everything. Outside forces like advertising are irrelevant.'

Not so. Nobody *needs* diamonds. The marketing challenge is to make people want them, which is tough, especially during a recession. Comparable advertised items, such as watches and gold jewellery with genuine functional worth or investment value, did not fare as well.

'Retail sales were strong before the advertising broke, they weren't going down and they would have kept going anyway despite the fall in consumer confidence.'

De Beers was still advertising using local creative work at that time, which was presumably having some impact. However, there is usually a lag between consumer confidence and sales, both in terms of decline and recovery. The power of the 'Shadows' campaign meant that sales did not follow the decline of consumer confidence but instead remained steady. This in turn encouraged the trade to stop de-stocking, start building up inventory again and offer the consumer more enticing jewellery pieces.

'The Asian economy never went into recession, in fact, the reverse. Those markets kept the whole thing buoyant.'

Japan had a deep recession. Hong Kong has 1997 to worry about. Other Asian markets are not strong diamond markets but are emerging. In 1994, the East Asia region accounted for only 17% of rough sales and, while this has almost doubled since 1980, its growth has been gradual over the entire period.

Estimating advertising contribution
Short Term – Linking Advertising to Retail Sales
The advertising has helped to separate the diamond industry's fortunes from the vicissitudes of consumer confidence levels, and maintain overall diamond jewellery market value stability. It has done this by:

- causing 'trade up' (in mature markets) by raising the average price paid, due to increased diamond content within the jewellery;
- building penetration in developing markets;
  - creating/reinforcing diamond occasions;
  - making strong partners of the jewellery trade;
- reassuring investors of the potential of the diamond market.

Long Term – Maintaining Image Saliency
The campaign has maintained (in some markets increased) the desirability of diamonds among consumers. The benefits of this will be manifest in future sales as they pass along the 'purchase pipeline'. In image terms, the advertising has made diamonds more special than gold and other precious gems, and reinforced their role as the ultimate gift of love, to help ensure that 'it' really is forever.

Overall, the campaign has scored highest-ever advertising awareness, recall and likeability for any campaign De Beers has ever run. The finished films have achieved extremely high standout and purchase interest scores in advertising pre-tests.

The future
Given the success to date, we are actively looking at a number of potential developing diamond markets – Vietnam, Argentina and Colombia – and the suitability of 'Shadows' to run there. We have launched 'Shadows' in Turkey this year, and continue to investigate other Middle Eastern markets such as Lebanon, Syria and Egypt. We are currently conducting a pilot advertising programme in Russia.

Thus, the De Beers 'Shadows' campaign continues to demonstrate its flexibility and adaptability to be effective in a wide variety of very different cultures, while promoting a range of diamond products in just about every market in the world.

Barclaycard: How a Bungling Secret Agent did More Than You'd Credit

Sarah Carter
(BMP DDB Needham, 1992)

There are few brand success stories in a recession. This is a striking example of an exception – and one in a market inextricably linked to total consumer spending where it would therefore perhaps least be expected. We are familiar with advertising 'adding value' to parity products. This paper shows the advertising contribution to a business through 'adding value' to a differentiated product, and, once the new product features had been communicated by letter, through converting this knowledge into the changes in attitudes and behaviour which turned round the brand's performance.

Background

Barclaycard was launched in 1966 – the first means of paying 'by plastic' with a rolling credit facility. Barclaycard had the market to itself until Access was launched in 1973. There followed a period of continuous, rapid and profitable growth in credit card marketing, and for Barclaycard, though Barclaycard's share of total turnover had fallen for many years as a result of other banks and building societies entering the market.

A Maturing Market

By 1989, a number of factors came together to cause a fundamental change in the market and, as a result, a total turnaround in Barclaycard's profitability.

Credit card issuers generate income and profit in two ways:

1. *Turnover-based income:* a proportion of each credit card transaction. The more cardholders spend on their credit cards, the more the issuer receives.

2. *Interest income:* interest paid by cardholders on the proportion of the monthly balance not paid off each month. The higher this proportion, the more the issuer receives in interest. It is the interest-paying cardholders who are the most profitable to any credit card issuer.

By the late 1980s Barclaycard faced a maturing market and, on top of this, a recession. Both turnover and interest income were hit.

Turnover Income
The long-term growth in credit card turnover ground to a halt as the economy entered recession. Debit cards, introduced in 1987, had also started to take off as a payment mechanism and therefore invade credit card territory. Barclaycard was still losing share, but now in a market that had stopped growing.

Interest Income
People were becoming increasingly wary of credit due to the recession, and more sophisticated in their use of credit cards. As a result, the profitable proportion of cardholders who regularly paid interest was declining, from 46% of the total to 37%, with full payers doubling from 17% to 34%.

The effect of these changes on Barclaycard was dramatic. In 1989, Barclays Central Retail Services Division (CRSD) saw profits fall by more than half compared with 1988, and in 1990 it made a loss.

1989: a new business strategy
Clearly, in a static market, Barclaycard needed to find a way to turn round and increase its share of turnover if it was to grow its business. There were two possible strategies: either to be cheaper than other credit cards or to be 'better'.

The first option, to become cheaper by cutting interest rates, was dismissed. Cardholders are remarkably unaware of comparative credit card interest rates and only a third of Barclaycard holders regularly paid interest, so this benefit was not widely relevant. Barclaycard decided to look at developing a 'better' product.

The Decision to Change the Product
By 1989, research revealed a market of parity products. Credit cardholders saw their cards as similar if not identical and, as a result, had little or no loyalty to any particular card. To grow share in a parity market, clearly the product needed to be different.

Barclaycard marketing decided to be brave. They would pursue a differentiation strategy by upgrading the Barclaycard product. They would also go one step further and charge an annual fee to provide an additional income stream (all credit cards were free at this time). Barclaycard would reposition itself as the superior mass-market credit card.

The New Product
It was obvious from the start that imposing a fee would inevitably lead to the loss of some cardholders, but research showed that these were more likely to be the full payers and the non-users – the most unprofitable of the customer segments. Interest-paying cardholders (the most profitable segment) reacted positively. On balance, the benefits of Barclaycard with the additional new feature outweighed what was a minimal cost.

Providing the new product was seen as offering value to enough cardholders in total to still benefit from economies of scale, the fee provided the opportunity to create a more profitable cardholder base.

Following some quantified validation, it was concluded that the optimum product mix was an annual fee of £8 combined with the following:

- A modest reduction in interest rates.
- Free purchase protection.
- A free international rescue service.
- The opportunity for Barclaycard Visa holders to apply for a free Barclaycard Mastercard. This card was linked to the Mastercard (as opposed to Visa) international network. It had a separate bill and credit limit and therefore helped to organise spending more effectively.

By April 1990, a new, differentiated product was in place from which to relaunch Barclaycard. The marketing objectives and strategy were set as follows:

Marketing objectives
Overall, to restore profitability for Barclaycard by:

- *Increasing turnover:* halt then reverse the long-term decline in share, from 30% and falling to 33% and rising by the end of 1992.

(Whilst 3% difference in share may not sound a lot, it is worth noting that 1% of turnover share was equivalent to about £280 million in 1990.)

– *Increasing new cardholders:* halt the decline then increase the share of new cardholders from 10% in 1989 to 15% by 1992 – a difficult objective, but vital to ensure Barclaycard's long-term success.

The New Barclaycard
The new product and fee were introduced and explained by letter to cardholders in May 1990, and were promoted in leaflets included with statements over the following months.

The new advertising campaign
Having changed the product, Barclaycard wished to develop new advertising, and appointed a new agency – BMP.

The Role for Advertising
Against the three marketing objectives the role for advertising was:

– *Restructuring the cardholder base.* To convince non 'die-hard' fee-averse customers of the increased value of a Barclaycard – hence cushioning the blow of the £8 fee and preventing them from leaving.
– *Increasing turnover.* To provide reasons why Barclaycard should be used in preference to other cards. If successful this would obviously increase Barclaycard's share of turnover.
– *Increasing new cardholders.* As fees were likely to become the norm of the credit card market (in fact most major credit cards did go on to charge a fee), it seemed clear that new cardholders would make a more considered choice than had been the case in the past (probably choosing only one credit card). Advertising had a significant role here to persuade potential new cardholders to choose a Barclaycard rather than some other card.

The Creative Brief
Who are we talking to? What do we want them to do?

– Existing Barclaycard holders. We want them to keep their Barclaycard and to use it more often than other cards.
– People considering a new credit card. We want them to choose a Barclaycard in preference to other cards.

What do we want to say to them?
Barclaycard is more than just another credit card.

Support
The new Barclaycard benefits (ie purchase protection, etc.).

Developing the Creative Idea

The new product benefits had been very well communicated by the direct mail activity, but this awareness was not translating into improved perceptions of Barclaycard, or into increased share of turnover. In fact, the decline in turnover actually accelerated.

We concluded that:

- We needed to talk about benefits not features. To do this we decided to show the features in action, and this meant a focus on one at a time.
- It seemed that turning these extra features into perceptions of a better product demanded adding an emotional dimension to our advertising – not trying to rationally persuade cardholders of Barclaycard's superiority. It therefore seemed very important that the advertising should be positively liked and enjoyed.

A New Creative Idea

This featured Rowan Atkinson as an opinionated yet bungling secret agent – Richard Latham – equipped for service with a Barclaycard but continually underestimating how it could help him out of a spot of bother.

Pre-testing confirmed that the idea could meet our objectives:

- The enjoyment and involvement with the idea could sweep aside cynicism, allowing people to believe our 'claims' of a superior product.
- The product features were reassessed as benefits.

This was in marked contrast to the response to the direct mail which had successfully communicated the different product, but had clearly achieved little by way of changing perceptions of Barclaycard as being a 'better' card.

Three executions of the new campaign idea were produced in December 1990: 'London' setting up the secret agent theme and restating the international acceptability benefit; 'Moscow' featuring the international rescue service and 'Cairo' featuring purchase protection. Barclaycard invested heavily in this campaign, at twice the previous level (1,750 TVRs in 1991 compared to 790 in 1990).

The Results

Barclaycard's share of new credit cardholders rose from 10% pre-advertising to 15% by December 1991 (post-advertising). Access share over the same period fell. The ambitious 15% share objective was therefore met – and a year ahead of plan. Importantly, Barclaycard's share of first-ever credit cardholders increased even more significantly, from 15% to 26%.

Overall, Barclaycard had emerged as turnover brand leader and growing, exceeding all its marketing objectives a year ahead of plan. People were increasingly keeping their Barclaycard rather than other cards, using their Barclaycard rather than other cards, and getting a new Barclaycard rather than other cards.

The effect of this performance on profitability was pronounced. Barclays CRSD's net loss in 1990 was transformed into a £46 million profit in 1991 (in the midst of one of Britain's longest recessions).

Proving the advertising effect: how the advertising worked

Advertising worked just as we planned.

Advertising Awareness

At the same time as Barclaycard doubled its Adspend, Access halved Adspend in response to the turbulent market conditions. As a result, Barclaycard's ad awareness increased from 13% before the first burst to 34% by the end of 1991, while Access declined over the same period from 30% to 20%.

Importantly, Barclaycard advertising awareness after just one year of the new campaign was nearly three times higher than that of Whicker in its first year (1982), at similar levels of TVRs, demonstrating the success of the new campaign in the difficult task of replacing a memorable advertising property.

Product Awareness

The advertising communicated the desired product messages extremely well. Awareness of the product changes rose steadily during advertising to exceed the levels achieved by the direct mail communication (Table 1).

TABLE 1: BARCLAYCARD PRODUCT AWARENESS

	% agreeing with statement			
	Post-DM/ pre-advertising Dec 1990	1st burst Mar 1991	2nd burst Jul 1991	3rd burst Dec 1991
Provides emergency assistance all over the world	37	39	47	58
Provides insurance cover on goods bought with the card	42	57	65	72

Source: Millward Brown
Base: All Barclaycard cardholders

Appeal

The new campaign rapidly established itself as one of the few that really grips the public's attention and affection, with levels of enjoyment three times higher and likeability six times higher than competitors' advertising. Highly appealing advertising was identified as important for success, but is a tough objective in the financial sector.

Imagery

Following the advertising breaking, people were beginning to view Barclaycard as not just different, but better (Table 2). This had not occurred after the direct mail.

TABLE 2: BARCLAYCARD IMAGE CHANGES

	% agreeing with statement			
	Post-DM/ pre-advertising Dec 1990	1st burst Mar 1991	2nd burst Jul 1991	3rd burst Dec 1991
Provides special benefits and services for its cardholders	38	42	59	66
Provides a high quality customer service	46	48	50	51
Cares for its customers' needs	34	36	50	52

Source: Millward Brown
Base: All Barclaycard cardholders

In addition, Barclaycard cardholders were increasingly rating their card dramatically more highly than Access holders' view of Access. We had created real 'daylight' between them as planned (Table 3).

TABLE 3: DIFFERENTIATION OF BARCLAYCARD FROM ACCESS

(Barclaycard cardholders' view of Barclaycard indexed against Access holders' view of Access)

	% agreeing with statement	
	Pre-advertising Dec 1990	Post-advertising Dec 1991
Provides special benefits and services for its cardholders	118	143
Provides a high quality customer service	112	124
Cares for its customers' needs	103	152

Source: Millward Brown

People who had both Access and Barclaycard had increased their preference for Barclaycard following the advertising. After a year of advertising, more than twice as many people (who held both a Barclaycard and an Access card) chose to keep Barclaycard rather than Access if they could only keep one.

Eliminating other variables
The New Product
Although the new features undoubtedly had an effect, it took advertising to gain significant leverage from these product changes. Despite the new product being in place, and people knowing about it, Barclaycard's turnover performance between June 1990 and the beginning of advertising in January 1991 showed little movement after the initial fall due to the fee introduction.

Simple comparisons of attitudinal trends with the introduction of the new product and the start of advertising showed no significant changes in Barclaycard's performance until after advertising. Nothing else changed in January and continued over the course of 1991 to explain why this should be so.

Finally, qualitative research had strongly suggested that the product changes alone were unlikely to change people's preference for Barclaycard in the way seen. The new features when presented 'raw' were usually met by suspicion and a feeling of 'no big deal'.

Reduction in Barclaycard Interest Rate

Econometric modelling has confirmed that relative credit card interest rates bear no relationship to turnover, either for Barclaycard or for the market as a whole. Besides, any effect would have resulted in share increases between June 1990 and December 1990. This did not occur.

Fee Level

It could be argued that a higher price in the form of the fee could somehow have raised quality perception of Barclaycard. Extensive research was conducted on the likely response to a fee before its introduction and there was no evidence that a higher price in any way raised perceptions. As we have seen, the reverse was true.

Other Possible Influences

There has been no change in any of the following:

- Outlet acceptability of Barclaycard.
- Amount or nature of the direct marketing activity by Barclaycard either to its existing cardholders or to potential new cardholders. (Indeed, if anything, recruitment activity by Barclaycard had been cut back in order to reduce the risk of taking on bad debts, the incidence of which increases in recession.)
- Profiles, the turnover-based points scheme, running for four years now.

We also know that the decline of Access advertising support in 1991 compared with 1990 did not occur until after October 1991. Not until December 1991, once Barclaycard's pattern of turnover growth was well established, could the year-on-year decline in Access advertising in 1991 have had any impact on Barclaycard's performance.

Thus we believe that for the majority of Barclaycard's success in 1991, we have proved that advertising alone was the cause.

Pay-back on advertising

Advertising was planned to generate additional profit in two ways:

- *Short-term:* advertising was planned to stimulate increased usage from Barclaycard holders and thereby turnover. Econometric analysis has shown that the advertising in 1991 was directly responsible for adding £508 million turnover to Barclaycard. As a result of the incremental profit this produced, the advertising investment in the short term alone paid for itself more than three times over.

- *Longer term:* advertising was designed to enhance the perceived value of Barclaycard, so that cardholders remain with Barclaycard (particularly important given that new cardholders take some years to become profitable) and new cardholders are attracted. This helps maintain:
  - a large cardholder base;
  - resistance to the emergent debit card market;
  - defence against possible future aggressive drives into the UK by foreign credit card issuers.

The longer term return on this investment is more difficult to directly quantify. But we can, as an example, calculate that if advertising helped to retain just 2% of Barclaycard's cardholders who otherwise would have been lost, the profit these would deliver over their 'lifetime' with Barclaycard would more than pay for the 1991 advertising investment.

The real contribution of our advertising to Barclaycard's profitability is therefore significantly higher than 1991 returns alone.

Summary and conclusions

In retrospect, it is easy to underestimate the magnitude of the success of Barclaycard in recovering from the desperate situation it faced back in 1989. It would have been tempting for it to take the lower risk route adopted by its competitors – simply taking more money from its cardholders in the form of a fee, without putting back value into the product through new features and advertising support.

Two principles have been demonstrated which were central to Barclaycard's success. It is difficult to see how Barclaycard could have increased its share of an undifferentiated market with a parity product. A differentiated product was the necessary starting point for growth. But even with a different product in place, it took advertising to provide leverage from the changes, translating the new product features into valued benefits, in a way which changed attitudes and behaviour and propelled Barclaycard to brand leader.

Second, however bad the market conditions, with investment both in the right product and aggressive advertising support, brands can adapt to remain successful and highly profitable. In fact, since these same conditions may encourage competitors to choose to pursue superficially safer strategies by cutting investment, bad times may create opportunities for the brave!

CASE 5

Love Over Gold: The Untold True Story of TV's Greatest Romance

Colin Flint
(McCann-Erickson, 1996)

> Gold Blend was launched by Nestlé in the mid-1960s. It used the new freeze-dried technology to provide a smoother, richer taste, and was sold at a price premium to Nescafé of around 25%. It was an excellent product, out-performing its rivals in taste tests, and was very successful in its early years. It reached a peak brand share of 7.8% in 1969, but thereafter drifted away slightly until, by the mid-1980s, the share was around 6.5%. This paper chronicles the creation and development of a new advertising campaign that revolutionised the Gold Blend brand over a ten-year period.

The strategic insight

Up to 1987, advertising had concentrated on the product itself, using the symbol of a gold bean to suggest product superiority. Thus the brand's appeal was limited to upmarket coffee connoisseurs.

Believing there was a bigger opportunity for the brand, the agency, McCann-Erickson, determined to create advertising which would make the brand more accessible to the mass market while still maintaining its quality, upmarket image and premium positioning. They therefore moved from product claims to a more emotional approach which involved the consumer more – Gold Blend would be the coffee you drank to demonstrate your sophistication. This was done by creating a sophisticated world you could become involved in and be part of. As such it could become a powerful brand to which anyone could relate.

There was also a change in tone. The previous advertising had featured Fiona Fullerton as a spokesperson. While aspirational, she reflected a strident feminism which many women found unappealing.

The brief for the new ads was for a softer form of feminism; a woman who was an equal in lifestyle, success and intellect, without being aggressive – a switch from material to more human values.

The creative insight

The task which the creative team set itself was to produce a campaign that was talked about as much as the programmes. Unusually, the stimulus for the creative idea came from the media plan. The size of the advertising budget for Gold Blend meant that two or three TV commercials a year would be needed. The team decided to present them sequentially as a series.

What were people talking about at the time on television? It was the upmarket series like *Dallas*, *Dynasty* and, more interesting to us, *Moonlighting*. This last programme featured two combative protagonists, who were clearly meant for each other. However, something always conspired to keep them apart. It was a sophisticated romance, and the theme appealed immensely to the women who were our target. This 'sophisticated romance' became the campaign theme.

We used trailers, advertisements and publicity to advertise each 'episode' of the campaign, just as TV companies did with TV series.

The media strategy complemented this approach, building on the drama of the romance rather than simply chasing cost per thousand. Most of the budget was spent on TV, using a burst strategy to emphasise the cliffhanger endings. Each burst began with a brief reminder of the previous episode. In the second week the new episode was launched, buying into high-rating programmes to build cover and impact. In the early stages of each series the story was moved on more quickly, with a faster production of episodes to get people involved in the story.

Advertising strategy

Target

Women of any class, who saw themselves as slightly more discriminating than the norm, but who were not coffee connoisseurs. For the second series a greater emphasis was put on younger women.

Objective

To position Gold Blend as an upmarket coffee, in a class of its own, worth every penny, but which anyone could drink.

To build an emotional bond between the target and the brand through the shared Gold Blend world of sophistication and romance.

And hence to broaden the appeal of the brand to new, less overtly upmarket, users.

Strategy
To involve the target in the world of Gold Blend where 'Classy women drink Gold Blend'.

Brand Image
Stylish good taste.

THE FIRST SERIES

THE SECOND SERIES

111

Campaign structure/media plan

The campaign broke in November 1987 with a burst of 700 TVRs, and it has generally had four bursts a year with about three executions a year.

From 1987–92, the media weight was maintained at around 3,000 TVRs a year. Since then it has declined slightly as the fame of the campaign has allowed it to run at lower weights without losing impact.

The first series was intended to run for six episodes. In the end, because it was so successful, it ran for 12 episodes over five and a half years. The first campaign drove penetration, mostly among the over-45s. For the second series this success was extended to younger women. A core objective of the new series was therefore to appeal to a younger target. The protagonists were younger, with more relevant lifestyle to this target, and more lively. The second series, introduced in 1993, was equally successful and is still running in 1996.

The campaign captured the public's imagination. It made the front page of the *Sun*, displacing the news that Princess Anne was having a romance with Tim Lawrence to second place, and was the subject of a *Times* editorial. The campaign used advertising in the TV listing pages to get people to tune in to watch the spot. When the first episode of the second series was shown in the centre break of *Brookside* and advertised in the listings pages, BARB saw a 67% increase in the number of people switching into the break compared to the week before. The campaign has also spawned a book, two CD/cassettes (one of which was gold) and a video, each successful and profitable in its own right for Nestlé and, at the same time, increasing the power of the campaign.

The *Love Over Gold* CD:	Straight into the Top 10 album charts
The *Love Over Gold* book:	Straight into the Top 10 bestsellers
Best of Gold Blend video:	Sold 1,500 copies (people actually bought copies of the ads!)

Sales effectiveness

Volume sales have grown by over 60% since 1987, despite a slight decline in the market as a whole. Gold Blend now has a sterling share of 13%, making it clearly the second largest brand in the market behind Nescafé granules. Significantly, the brand continued growing during the recession years of 1988–92 (Figure 1).

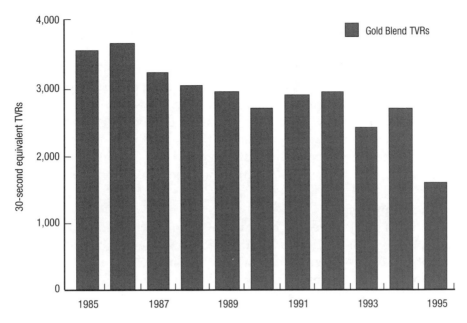

FIGURE 1: GOLD BLEND SALES VOLUME

What else could have caused the sales increase?
Price
What matters in this market is price relative to the competition. Nescafé as brand leader with 40% of the market sets the prices. While actual prices have varied with commodity prices, Gold Blend's relative price versus Nescafé and Kenco has remained unchanged, except for short-term variations which reflect promotional activity or the phasing of price increases.

Distribution
Distribution for Gold Blend was good even in 1986–87 at 90% sterling. Distribution has not been a significant factor in the brand's success.

Competitive Activity
Like any successful brand, Gold Blend's success has encouraged rivals. Most, for example, Maxwell House Master Blend and Maxwell House Classic, failed. The most successful were Kenco and supermarkets' own-brand freeze-dried.

Kenco was launched in 1988 at the same price as Gold Blend. It rapidly reached a brand share of just under 3%, growing to 3.7% with a further 2.7% coming from line extensions. Despite what was undoubtedly a successful competitive launch, Gold Blend continued to

113

grow through this period, only plateauing in 1992. Moreover, with the launch of the second series in 1993, Gold Blend's growth has resumed and Kenco's has been halted.

Own-label activity has largely concentrated on price promotions, and in this context most of the supermarkets have been pursuing a policy of selling direct equivalents of Gold Blend, some of which look very like Gold Blend. This activity has been an almost constant factor and has, if anything, increased in recent years.

Thus, since 1987, the competitive context for Gold Blend has got tougher rather than easier, partly in response to Gold Blend's success.

Product Improvements

Nestlé takes great pride in the quality of its products, and undoubtedly the quality of Gold Blend has been a major factor in its success. Indeed a basic theme of this paper is that it was the combination of a good product and powerful and appropriate brand advertising from 1987 that has created Gold Blend's success.

Gold Blend has existed since the mid-1960s and has always done well in blind product tests. However, it was only when the new advertising was introduced in 1987 that sales started to take off.

Since 1987 the product has seen a number of improvements. However, what these have done is to maintain the brand's lead over its competitors, who have also been improving their products. In addition, all the most significant improvements were also introduced by Nescafé, which has not seen comparable growth levels.

Packaging

While Gold Blend was the first brand to move to a square jar, this packaging format has since been copied, particularly by private labels, and is not seen by consumers as a major part of its appeal. Gold Blend's packaging has not changed significantly during the campaign.

Can we show a direct link between the advertising and sales?

Unfortunately, regional testing was ruled out at an early stage, both because of Nestlé's desire to build on its success nationally, but also because of the nature of the contracts with the TV companies. Similarly, because of the success of the campaign there was no prolonged period off-air.

However, two special analyses were conducted: AGB's MediaSpan and an econometric analysis of sales.

MediaSpan

AGB's MediaSpan provides a link between an individual's viewing of advertising and their purchasing, and is available for 1993–95. This allows us to quantify advertising's short-term contribution to sales. Specifically it answers the question, 'Are people who have seen our advertising in the last two weeks more likely to buy Gold Blend than those who have not?' This shows:

- there is a strong correlation between exposure to advertising and purchase. People who had seen one or more ad in the last two weeks bought 14% more Gold Blend than those who had not;
- the advertising works more strongly when combined with favourable pricing. With low pricing it increases volume by up to 20%. When it is higher the advertising still works, but needs more exposures (three) and even then has a smaller effect (+7%).

As well as these short-term effects, MediaSpan also found evidence of a longer-term effect with a significant difference in Gold Blend's brand share between heavy viewers (who had therefore been exposed to more Gold Blend advertising over the years) and light viewers. The effect is strongest among the 16–44 age group, who became a particular target for the second series, which started in November 1993.

Econometric Analysis

An econometric analysis of Gold Blend's sales shows a similar picture, with advertising being one of the main drivers of sales, along with price and promotions. The effect is such that 835 TVRs of advertising create a short-term increase of 25 tonnes, about a 9% increase in monthly sales.

Business effect

The advertising is not cost-effective in the short term. At a simple level sales growth has averaged around £6 million a year, little more than the advertising spend at £5 million. However, this growth has been compound and consistent. New buyers brought in through the advertising have become loyal buyers; 45% of new buyers of Gold Blend in 1994 and 1995 went on to become repeat buyers (source: AGB). This compound effect means that Gold Blend sales are now (1996) worth £50 million a year in real terms more than they were prior to the start of the campaign in 1987. Average advertising expenditure on Gold Blend across the period was £5 million a year.

How did the advertising work?

The advertising was highly memorable, with 63% aware of it at its peak and 48% able to recall details (source: tracking study). In 1989, 1990 and 1991 it was the second most memorable campaign on *Marketing's* Adwatch survey of all brands in all categories, and has been consistently in the Top 10 in other years.

Qualitative research showed that, as planned, the advertising worked by portraying an upmarket, sophisticated image for Gold Blend that, because of the populist nature of the advertising, was accessible to everyone. This appeals because the image is aspirational for our target and, at a rational level, communicates quality: *'If people like that drink it it must be good.'* The popular appeal of the advertising means that people accept these messages, even though they know the characters are advertising inventions. They go along with the fantasy because they enjoy it.

Quantitatively we find that people – especially ABC1s, but also many C2DEs – say that Gold Blend is an 'upmarket' coffee with advertising they like. The result is that Gold Blend now appeals to a broad range of people, while still maintaining its upmarket image. Brand penetration has expanded most among C2DEs, who previously found the product appealing but the brand inaccessible.

As previously stated, a secondary aim of the second series, which started in November 1993, was to create more appeal among younger people. As well as the MediaSpan analysis this is shown in penetration growth. Between 1986 and 1993, penetration (drinking yesterday, source: NDS) grew by 46% among over-45s, but only by 4% among under-45s. Since 1993 the pattern has changed. From 1993 to 1996 penetration grew by 15% among under-45s and 14% among over-45s. This has been confirmed in the tracking study data, where the advertising, while liked by everyone, has stronger appeal for younger respondents and is the only advertising in this market to generate real involvement.

How did it affect the rest of the portfolio?

During the period of Gold Blend's success, Nescafé as a brand performed roughly in line with the market, while some of the other new Nestlé brands – Alta Rica, Cap Colombie and Cappuccino – actually increased share. Thus the growth in Gold Blend's share was all incremental for Nestlé, and was achieved without cannibalising the other brands in the portfolio. This is despite advertising weights which were lower (eg Nescafé averaged 6,000 TVRs pre-1987 and 5,000 since compared to Gold Blend's 2,500–3,000 TVRs). Surprisingly, there was no trading down to the cheaper Nescafé during the recession years.

International success

Although Nestlé believes in local advertising solutions, the Gold Blend campaign has proved capable of crossing borders. In most cases, re-shot using local actors, it has run successfully in the US, Canada, Denmark, Norway, Sweden, Finland and Chile.

Summary

Since the launch of this campaign, Gold Blend has almost doubled its market share and grown from a minor player to the second largest coffee brand and one of the country's Top 50 brands. This success has been sustained over nearly ten years, with each year building on the previous one.

Moreover, this was not chance, but came from the aim of creating an accessible 'upmarket' brand, and the ambition to be more like the programmes between which the advertising appeared.

The increased size of the brand is worth £50 million each year in sales, at a cost on average of £5 million a year in advertising spend. Furthermore, this does not represent increased advertising spend, merely a more effective use of that money. To quote David Hudson, Communications Director of Nestlé UK:

> *'It is a campaign I take real pride in. Sometimes people ask me if the amount we spend on advertising is worth it. I tell them to look at the Gold Blend campaign.'*

BMW: How 15 Years of Consistent Advertising Helped BMW Treble Sales Without Losing Prestige

Tim Broadbent
(WCRS, 1994)

This case shows how consistent advertising for BMW over a long period of time has built an exceptionally strong brand which has sustained the business performance through good times and in bad.

BMW's business objectives

BMW (GB) was established in 1979 as a wholly owned subsidiary of BMW (AG). It replaced a distributor which also sold other 'performance' marques such as Maserati. Its objective was to treble volume sales by 1990 (from 13,000 new cars a year to 40,000) while maintaining profit margins.

Advertising objectives

WCRS was appointed in 1979 and began the 'Ultimate Driving Machine' campaign which is still running.

A primary advertising objective was to create a richer brand image. BMWs were mainly known as performance cars, reflecting the models imported in the 1970s. It was necessary to reach beyond the 'enthusiast' consumer segment in order to achieve the sales target. A secondary objective was to improve BMW's reputation as prestige cars, even though people would see more of the less exclusive models on the road as sales grew.

The advertising strategy which met these objectives
BMW's strategy has been shaped by four concepts: core brand values, sniper strategy, centre of gravity and BMW tone of voice.

Core Brand Values
Research indicates that the BMW brand is selected before individual models. In the past, the brand was very demanding of its driver as he was expected to share the potency of its performance imagery. Broadening its image allowed more types of drivers to desire BMW and rationalise its high price. Increasing the brand's prestige helped sell more affordable models; as a younger marque than Mercedes or Jaguar, BMW at that point lacked the prestige conferred by heritage.

> *'A BMW doesn't give me any prestige to arrive outside the Polygon Hotel in, I'll be honest. The BMW is not – well, the mechanics are brilliant, but it does nothing for me.'*

> *'I regard that Mercedes have had a quality motor car for a good while, and BMW are trying very hard to catch up the Mercedes image. But they are a younger company who are coming along behind a position that Mercedes have been in for a while.'*

(Car clinic qualitative research,
Communications Research Ltd, July 1980)

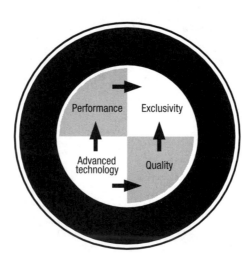

FIGURE 1: BMW CORE BRAND VALUES

Consumer research and 'product interrogation' with BMW engineers in Germany ('interrogating the product until it confesses to its strengths' is a cornerstone in the WCRS strategic process) identified four core brand values. These values shape all BMW communications, though their expression in advertising has evolved in response to social, economic, environmental and competitive changes (Figure 1).

- *Performance:* has evolved from 'cars which go faster' to 'cars which are rewarding to drive', as pure 0–60mph acceleration has become less relevant (and socially acceptable) in today's driving conditions.
- *Quality:* has evolved from 'cars which are well made' to 'quality which permeates every aspect of BMW ownership, from initial design through to servicing', as standards of car construction have risen among all manufacturers.
- *Advanced technology:* has evolved from 'the latest technology' to 'the most relevant and thoughtful technology', as other manufacturers – particularly Japanese – have packed their cars with hi-tech gizmos.
- *Exclusivity:* the product of these values, has evolved from 'rarity and snob value' to 'values not available elsewhere; only BMW could make a car like this', as the number of BMWs seen on the road has increased.

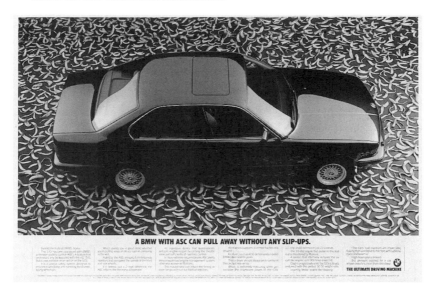

A BMW WITH ASC CAN PULL AWAY WITHOUT ANY SLIP-UPS.

The evolution of core values ensured that BMW, the ultimate yuppie driving machine of the 1980s, remains a relevant and socially acceptable brand in the recessionary 1990s.

Sniper Strategy

BMW advertising in Britain is notable for the production of a large number of different advertisements every year. Each ad shows a different aspect of core brand values, aimed at a particular group in the marketplace, hence the term 'sniper' strategy.

Research is used to identify particular groups of prospective customers and to establish which attributes are most important to them. For example, an ad about quality would help sell a 3 Series to an older man who values this attribute most, while an ad about 3 Series performance would be more attractive to a successful young executive.

Since 1979, 253 colour advertisements in leisure and weekend magazines, and – more recently – 24 television commercials, all reflecting core values, have created a richer image for BMW in Britain than elsewhere. This approach is different from other car advertisers, who make fewer advertisements and show each one more often. But BMW cars are not mass-produced, so neither are BMW advertisements.

Centre of Gravity

This concept recognises that the BMW brand is made up of many models varying dramatically in price and performance but sharing a driving experience that can be identified as BMW (Figure 2).

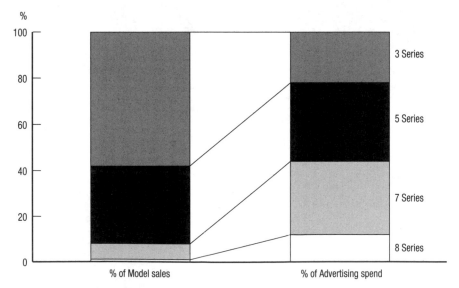

FIGURE 2: RAISING THE BRAND'S CENTRE OF GRAVITY
Base: 1990, a typical year which had no major new car launches

Placing greater advertising emphasis than sales warrant on more advanced models raises the centre of gravity (average perception) of the brand higher. This benefits the less expensive models in the range by adding to the intangible desirability of owning a BMW; it militates against hard-nosed comparisons of price/specification/performance with 'ordinary' cars. For example, a BMW 316i buyer would currently have to spend an extra £2,000 to match competitive specification, and he could easily choose a faster car at the price, but then he would not own 'a BMW'.

Many ads have stressed the similarities between the less expensive and more expensive models in the range.

BMW Tone of Voice

The BMW advertising produced over the years by WCRS looks and feels remarkably similar because of its consistent tone of voice.

- The 'BMW world' is not warm.
- There are few humans or signs of humans, because humanity can suggest fallibility, whereas BMWs are shown as precise, cold, technical icons with jewel-like perfection.
- The car is the master of each ad. The advertising idea is based on facts about the car.
- The art direction is a neutral frame in which the idea exists. There are no contrivances to add superficial glamour, such as stately homes, sunsets or glamorous blondes.
- Assumptive wit is used to puncture pomposity and create a feeling of belonging to the 'BMW club' among those who enjoy the joke.

These values have been consistent across all BMW communications, creating a campaign that is better known than would be predicted from BMW's relatively modest advertising budget. Since 1980, BMW has spent £91 million on advertising (at MEAL prices), which is a modest sum against sales of £6.3 billion.

Summary of BMW's Advertising Strategy Since 1979

BMW (GB) approached the challenge of trebling sales volume at high margins by using advertising to build the BMW brand. It changed the perception of BMWs from performance cars to a richer view of the brand through an advertising strategy that concentrated on the four core concepts: core brand values, sniper strategy, centre of gravity and consistent tone of voice. The question is: Did this strategy work for the business? In the following sections we show that it did.

BMW's business success

BMW (GB) set out to treble sales and to achieve growth with high profit margins. This has been achieved. Market share has also trebled, as BMW sales out-performed the market.

What are the causes of BMW's exceptional sales success? To answer this question we shall first show that price, distribution and improved products could not be solely responsible for BMW's sales success; then we shall show that richer brand imagery, created through advertising, has generated exceptionally strong consumer demand.

Factors which could not explain BMW's sales success

Price

BMW's sales have not trebled because of lower prices. German cars have become more expensive in Britain as the deutschmark has risen over sterling. The strength of the brand allowed BMW price increases even during the recession, unlike the market as a whole. Neither were BMW's price increases due to selling a higher proportion of expensive models: prices have risen even though BMW is selling proportionately more of its less expensive models.

Distribution

BMW's sales have not trebled because distribution trebled. The number of BMW dealers has increased by only 10% (though the quality of BMW dealerships has continually improved). However, BMW's rate of sale has overtaken the market average rate of sale, reflecting growing consumer demand for BMWs.

Improved Products

BMW's sales have not trebled because the products improved. Although the same improved BMWs are on sale throughout Europe, BMW's sales growth in Britain has out-performed BMW's sales growth in Germany, France and Italy. In 1980, Britain was the fourth largest market for BMWs in Europe (after Germany, France and Italy); by 1993, the British market was second only to Germany.

The strength of the BMW brand in Britain

The total number of BMWs on the road has increased from 81,000 in 1980 to 455,000 in 1993. The BMW 3 Series alone now sells more than all Audis and Saabs combined. One would expect that as BMW lost exclusivity, in reality it would come to be seen as a more ordinary car. However, BMW *imagery* has improved and it has become perhaps the strongest marque in Britain. A dedicated tracking study shows that BMW now has the strongest overall image of any major car brand, stronger even than Mercedes on key attributes; and an international image study commissioned by BMW (AG) shows that Britain is the only market in which BMW is more highly regarded than Mercedes (Figure 3).

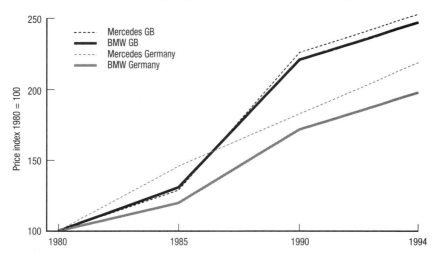

FIGURE 3: GERMAN CAR PRICE RISES IN BRITAIN VS. GERMANY
Base: 1980–94, BMWs and Mercedes 200/300
Source: *Auto Motor and Sport* (Germany); *What Car?* (Britain)

BMW's richer image in Britain has not been achieved through the model mix: the profile of model sales in the UK is very similar to that in France and Italy.

In 1979, BMW in Britain had weaker imagery than BMW in Germany (the home market is invariably stronger). But by 1992–93 BMW imagery in Britain at least matched BMW in Germany, while BMW's imagery in other markets has fallen relatively further behind BMW's imagery in Germany.

The strength of the brand has created exceptional consumer loyalty. For example, BMW and Audi are almost equally reliable cars, yet BMW owners are much more likely to repurchase than Audi owners and thus forgive the problems experienced (Table 1).

TABLE 1: CUSTOMERS' LOYALTY VS. PROBLEMS WITH CAR

	BMW	Audi
Average number of problems per owner	1.02	1.03
Previous car was same make (%)	58.00	37.00

Source: 1993 New Car Buyers' Survey

Qualitative research explains how the brand helps BMW owners 'forgive' any problems with their cars:

> *'If I'd had these experiences with a Rover, I'd think "Typical". As it's a BMW, I think I'm unlucky.'*

(Cragg Ross Dawson, The BMW Brand, March 1994)

BMWs have become symbols of success, not just sportiness. This gives new models a flying start in consumer appeal, as motoring journalists know:

> *'The Golf has a 10 bhp advantage and it's also better specified, with a standard electric sunroof, trip computer and a decent stereo – but it doesn't have BMW's coveted "spinning prop" badge.'*

(Re BMW Compact: *Top Gear*, April 1994)

Dealers now believe BMW is simply the best franchise to have in the whole market (see Figure 4).

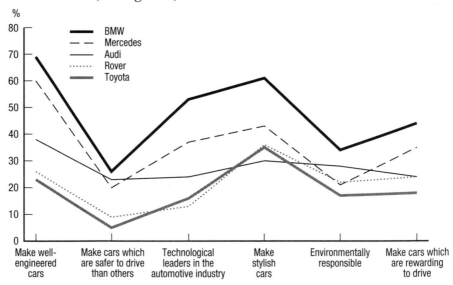

FIGURE 4: BMW'S BRAND IMAGE STRENGTHS
Source: Harris Research, April 1994

In conclusion, price, distribution and better products could not explain how BMW trebled sales in Britain. It is the exceptional richness of the brand that has created exceptionally strong consumer demand.

The next question is how advertising consistency helped create such a strong brand.

How advertising consistency created an exceptionally strong brand

A minor benefit of advertising consistency is that the campaign becomes known; BMW's advertising is much better known than would be expected on its relatively modest budget (smaller than Proton's, for example) (Figure 5).

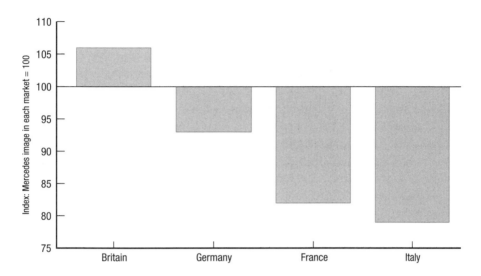

FIGURE 5: BMW IMAGERY VS. MERCEDES, 1992–93
Base: Average of 18 product image diverse cars
Source: International BMW Study 1992–93, Dr Salcher, Team GmbH

The fundamental benefit is what the fact of consistency signals to consumers about the company which is responsible for the cars and how they are advertised. It signals that BMWs are made by a group of people who have 'a distinctive philosophy', 'a certain mindset', 'a certain way of doing things to achieve a certain goal'. It signals that BMW has a view of how quality cars ought to be. Consumers believe that BMWs are good because BMW single-mindedly sets out to make good cars; that BMW unswervingly follows its vision of what a good car is; that BMW puts the manufacture of what it sees as good cars above all other considerations. In research, no other car manufacturer, not even Mercedes, comes across as being so dedicated to the art of making really desirable cars. (Source: Cragg Ross Dawson, The BMW Brand, March 1994.)

This impression of dedicated determination has been created by the consistency with which BMW has advertised the excellence of its cars for 15 years.

The value of the BMW brand

'You pay £9,000 for the car and £5,000 for the badge.'

(Competitive car owner, 1990)

It has been shown that since 1979 BMW prices rose higher than market prices; BMW's distribution rose by only 10%; and yet sales trebled, which is a much higher rate of growth than other European markets which sold the same cars. It has also been shown that the BMW brand in Britain is stronger than it was in 1979; is now stronger than other leading marques such as Mercedes; that Britain is the only market in which BMW is stronger than Mercedes; and that Britain is the only market in which the brand has become as strong as it is in Germany, if not stronger.

The only reasonable explanation for BMW's sales success in Britain is that the exceptional strength of the brand has created exceptionally strong consumer demand; and it has been explained how the consistency of BMW's advertising has created the impression of a company dedicated to the manufacture of good cars.

So, what is the cash value of the extra strength of the brand in Britain, and what is its relationship to the cost of the advertising, which helped create the extra brand strength?

There are two empirical methods of estimating how much of BMW's sales are due to the strength of the brand. First, suppose that BMW had average rate of sales increases – the same as the market rate of sale increases over the period 1980–93. Second, suppose that BMW sales in Britain had grown at the same rate as they did in Germany, France and Italy over the period 1980–93.

Calculating BMW's hypothetical sales under both of these suppositions eliminates some of the variables which would mask how much influence the stronger brand has had on sales. The effect of product improvements is eliminated in the comparison between other countries and Britain, because all markets received the same improved products. The effect of economic recession hitting European car markets at different times is eliminated in the average market rate of sale comparison, because the recession in Britain hit BMW at the same time as other marques.

Figures 6 and 7 show what volume sales would have been under both suppositions, compared to actual volume sales.

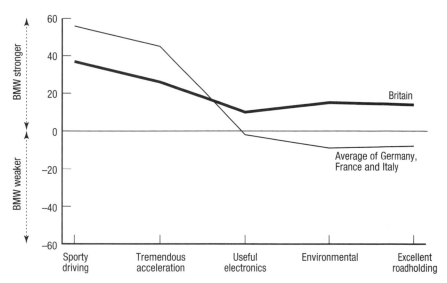

FIGURE 6: BMW'S RICHER BRAND IMAGERY IN BRITAIN. DIFFERENCES
BETWEEN BMW AND MERCEDES IMAGE RATINGS

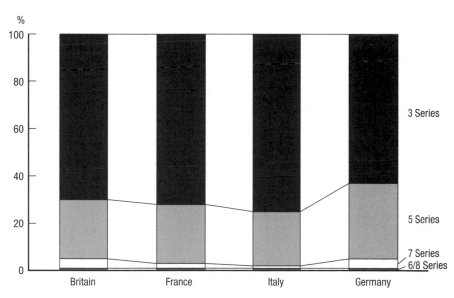

FIGURE 7: BMW SALES PROFILES IN BRITAIN, FRANCE, ITALY AND
GERMANY IN 1993

129

It can be seen that in both cases sales would have been significantly lower. Table 2 shows how much sales revenue would have been lost.

TABLE 2: SALES REVENUE

	Actual sales 1980–93	If... BMW's rate of sale increased at the same rate as all cars' rate of sale	If... BMW had same sales growth as in Germany, France and Italy
Sales volume	466,327	263,989	255,440
Sales value*	£6.3bn	£3.6bn	£3.1bn
Actual sales higher by...	–	£2.7bn	£3.2bn

* Total sales value 1980-93 divided by total sales volume gives average BMW car price over this period: £13,251

It can be seen that the extra strength of the BMW brand has probably been worth around £2.7 billion to £3.2 billion in extra sales over the past 15 years. These numbers are so large and surprising that it may be worth repeating that only two reasonable assumptions have been tested: that BMW could have had an average rate of sale increases, or that BMW could have had the same sales growth as in other major European markets. What these calculations do not allow for is improvements in dealer quality. There is no way to quantify dealer quality over time and across markets; it can therefore only be assumed to be a constant for these calculations.

However, improvements in dealer quality generally relate to better conversions of prospects to sales. What advertising does is to deliver new prospects in the first place. In 1993, for example, BMW's advertising created 35,000 enquiries, nearly all from non-customers, which helped the previous dealers sell to the 14,600 new customers won the previous year. So far this year (to 20 May 1994) advertising has been responsible for 99% of dealers' 'hot' and 'medium' prospects.

Conclusion

This case shows that BMW's advertising set out to enrich the brand's appeal, and that this has happened, and only in Britain, and that only in Britain have sales trebled.

BMW's advertising expenditure through WCRS has been £91 million. As this has helped create brand values worth some £3 billion in extra sales, the value of BMW's brand-building campaign seems beyond question.

Conclusions

Patrick Barwise

The central argument of this book is that:

1. Regardless of economic conditions, firms need a clear strategy for their major brands based on the classic marketing principles of segmentation, competitor analysis, understanding of their own competitive strengths, targeting, and positioning.
2. Advertising strategy should be an integral part of this wider strategy, not something separate, but should also have its own clear objectives.
3. As background to resource allocation, it can be useful to know the general patterns found in previous research represented in the six readings in Part One. On the specific question of advertising when the economy slows down, the research shows that the most successful companies tend to maintain or increase their advertising investment during recession and gain substantial increases in market share and profit during the recovery. Despite limitations in the research, this pattern of successful firm behaviour is well established.
4. Maintaining or increasing marketing investment when the economy slows down tends to reduce short-term financial performance. But crucially, it need not reduce the share price. Financial analysts and investors are well aware of the value of brand equity. They do not typically monitor the firm's advertising expenditure, but they have no problem supporting a firm which sacrifices short-term financial performance if this increases long-term shareholder value – and if they believe that the management has a convincing strategy. In other words, there is no major conflict between the need for a good strategy for business reasons and the need for such a strategy to persuade analysts and investors to support the firm's investment in marketing.
5. All this needs to be in the specific context of the firm, its brand(s), its markets and competitors, as well as general economic conditions. In marketing, the specifics are everything.

6. As illustrated by the six IPA cases in Part Two, successful advertising is not about just throwing money at the problem. As noted in (2), it is part of a wider strategy, involving excellent planning, execution, and subsequent evaluation.

The cases in Part Two also illustrate a number of other points:

–   Successful advertising is usually linked with excellent product quality and innovation. The effect is multiplicative. Advertising succeeds most when the product or service is good; but also, the success of a high-quality product can be greatly increased by good advertising which increases the product's *perceived* quality and emotional appeal.
–   Most successful campaigns are based on a deep understanding of the key drivers of consumer purchases within the target segment. Typically, this understanding revolves around a few powerful insights, not a long list of attributes.
–   However, successful campaigns also involve a strong emphasis on measuring both behavioural and attitudinal effects. These measures enable management to see that the advertising is working as planned and help to support the further development of the strategy and execution.
–   Although advertising evaluation tends to emphasise sales volumes and market shares, successful advertising often also supports premium prices. The cases we have chosen for Part Two are all for brands which were either premium-priced or (in the case of Whipsnade) increased price during a recession. Other things being equal, recessions favour brands that compete on price. In these cases, however, the advertising enabled the brand to buck this trend.
–   Finally, the most successful campaigns are also based on outstanding advertising (ie creative strategy and execution). In two of the six cases (Clio and Gold Blend), the advertising itself was so well executed and so emotionally compelling that it generated substantial unpaid media coverage in its own right.

As well as illustrating the general arguments, the cases should also be a source of inspiration, reminding us that successful strategy and marketing come from ideas, not just from techniques.

Three positive strategies

When the economy slows down, there are three generic positive responses:

1. *Look for new creative, targeting, or media opportunities:* In some contexts, the slower market conditions create new opportunities to emphasise different consumer benefits or segments. (For instance, as already noted, higher interest rates shift savings and disposable income from the under-fifties to the over-fifties.) Alternatively, tough times can provide the stimulus to think more creatively. Three of the cases in Part Two (Renault Clio, Whipsnade, and De Beers) describe firms getting imaginative when the going gets tough. Several of the strategies in Reading 6 (Broadbent) also fall under this heading.

2. *Strengthen your market position against weaker rivals:* The research shows clearly that the strongest, most successful firms can use the opportunity of an economic slowdown to attack their weaker rivals. One of the cases (Barclaycard) is about this strategy: Barclaycard gained significant market share during the early 1990s recession by investing in advertising while its main rival, Access, cut back. Simon Broadbent calls this strategy 'No more Mr Nice Guy'.

3. *Keep going:* Arguably, this is the best strategy of all. It is based on the idea that long-term shareholder value comes from excellent strategy executed consistently over many years. The last two cases (Gold Blend and BMW) reflect this strategy. The concerns about recession – that consumers may spend less on the category, that short-term financial performance may be under pressure – are balanced by the advantages – that the same Adspend gives a higher share of voice and that the financial markets will support a long-term strategy if they find it credible.

In one sense, the need for a distinctive, credible strategy has nothing to do with the state of the economy. But an economic slowdown can bring the issues to a head. This can be the opportunity to sharpen the discussion about marketing strategy in general. Deciding how much to spend on advertising should be just a part of that wider discussion.

About the Editor

Professor Patrick Barwise is Director of the Centre for Marketing at London Business School. The Centre acts as a vehicle for research by the marketing faculty at LBS and as a resource for the leading companies that support its work. Professor Barwise joined LBS in 1976, having spent his early career with IBM.

His previous publications include *Television and its Audience* (with Andrew Ehrenberg), *Accounting for Brands* (with Chris Higson, Andrew Likierman and Paul Marsh), *Strategic Decisions* (coedited with Vassilis Papadakis) and *Predictions: Media* (with Kathy Hammond). Current projects include a book with Andrea Dunham on *The Business of Brands*, to be published by Harvard Business School Press, the second edition of the television book, and chairing the *Future Media Research Programme* at LBS, funded by a consortium of 50 companies.

Patrick Barwise is also Deputy Chairman of Consumers' Association and Joint Managing Editor of *Business Strategy Review*.